Florida Gun Laws

Open, Concealed & Constitutional Carry

First Edition

By

LARRY E. HOLTZ, Esq.

Blue360°
Media

www.blue360media.com
To contact Blue360° Media, LLC, please call: **1-844-599-2887**

ISBN: 978-1-60885-774-6
eBook: 978-1-60885-775-3

Blue360° Media, LLC
2750 Rasmussen Rd., Suite 101
Park City, Utah 84098
1-844-599-2887
www.blue360media.com

(Pub. 80190)

IMPORTANT RESOURCES FOR FLORIDA LAW ENFORCEMENT OFFICERS

This publication is dedicated to all the brave men and women in uniform. We honor the people who work tirelessly to preserve our liberties and who make America the greatest Nation on Earth.

The information contained in this publication should not be construed as legal advice and should not be used as a substitute for independent legal research. Although we have made every effort to ensure that the information in this book was accurate and up to date at press time, whenever in doubt, consult with your local, state or federal authorities.

Table Of Contents

About the Author

Larry E. Holtz, Esq. received his Bachelor of Arts Degree in Criminal Justice from Temple University in Philadelphia, Pennsylvania, graduating Summa Cum Laude. He received his Juris Doctorate from Temple University School of Law, graduating in the top ten percent of his class.

Formerly a Sergeant of Detectives with the Atlantic City Police Department, an assistant county prosecutor, and a Deputy Attorney General, Mr. Holtz is presently an attorney specializing in criminal law and procedure. He has served as the Municipal Prosecutor for several towns, and as the Director of Holtz Learning Centers, a professional law enforcement school for continuing legal and criminal justice education and training.

During his tenure at the Attorney General's Office, he also served as a police instructor with numerous police academies, taught at two universities, including Widener University School of Law in Delaware, and Rowan University in Glassboro, New Jersey. He is a member of the Bar in New Jersey, Pennsylvania, and the District of Columbia.

Mr. Holtz is the author of *Criminal Procedure for Law and Justice Professionals,* the *New Jersey Law Enforcement Handbook* (3 Volume set), the *Pennsylvania Law Enforcement Handbook, Criminal Evidence for Law and Justice Professionals, Effective Law Enforcement Report Writing,* and the co-author of the *Texas Criminal and Traffic Procedural Manual,* and *Incident Response for Special Needs Populations,* along with a *Special Needs Instructor Implementation Guide.* He is also the author of various exam study guides for criminal law, search and seizure, and administrative policy and procedure. He is published in the *Pennsylvania Law Journal-Reporter,* the *Journal of Criminal Law and Criminology,* and the *Dickinson Law Review.*

PREFACE

RULE #1: Treat every firearm as if it's loaded and to always point it in a safe direction.

RULE #2: ***Never forget rule number one!***

You've made the decision to carry, and this text will guide you through everything you need to know—not just about finding the right carry rig (gun and holster) but also about equipping yourself with the knowledge to act confidently and lawfully in any situation.

Understanding what is legally allowed or required is essential for your safety and freedom, and it is the goal to provide you with a solid legal and practical foundation. The book goes beyond the basics often covered in a standard concealed carry class, which can sometimes be rushed or filled with distractions. The focus is to make the laws and protocols for open and concealed carry easier to understand, and to help you navigate the complexities of carrying a firearm with confidence and clarity. The text provides practical, straightforward information that will boost your confidence and open your mind to important considerations you may not have thought about.

Carrying a concealed firearm is a significant responsibility, and I commend you for taking the initiative to educate yourself beyond the brief training typically provided during a certification course. This shows your commitment to safety, preparedness, and responsible gun ownership.

If you're carrying under Florida's permitless carry law, this guide is even more essential. While you may not be required to hold a permit, understanding the laws, best practices, and your rights is crucial. This text should fill in the gaps, offering insights on everything from legal guidelines, situational awareness and case studies, to choosing the right equipment and preparing for different scenarios.

Think of this guide as your companion—something to which you can refer, learn from, and rely on. Whether you're new to concealed carry or have years of experience, the aim is to help you become a more informed and responsible armed citizen, ready for any situation.

Chapter One
Introduction

Carrying a firearm is a significant responsibility, and safety must always come first. Throughout this book, you'll be reminded of RULE #1: Treat every firearm as if it's loaded and always point it in a safe direction. RULE #2: Never forget rule number one! You've made the decision to carry, and this text will guide you through everything you need to know—not just about finding the right carry rig (gun and holster) but also about equipping yourself with the knowledge to act confidently and lawfully in any situation.

The phrase *"Constitutional Carry"* has been gaining popularity in states, including Florida, that do not require a permit or license to carry a handgun. It is a testimonial to the US Constitution's Second Amendment, with supporters pointing to the text of the constitutional provision as their "permit" or "license" to carry a handgun.

Constitutional carry generally means that the state's law does not prohibit citizens *who can legally possess a firearm* from carrying handguns (openly and/or in a concealed manner). The key phrase in that sentence is "legally possess." For example, a state can enact its own requirements as to who can openly carry a handgun. This includes regulations on things like the gun owner's age, residency, location, criminal history, and other potential factors. Thus, even if you live in a constitutional carry state, we recommend that you learn the state and local regulations before you start carrying your guns wherever you go.

Understanding the law is essential for your safety and freedom, and it is our goal to provide you with a solid legal foundation; the text goes beyond the basics often covered in a standard concealed carry class, which can sometimes be rushed or filled with distractions. Feel free to dog-ear, highlight, and make notes in this book to help reinforce key points that resonate with you.

At present, many states are re-examining their firearms carry laws in light of several important United States Supreme Court decisions.

These include *McDonald v. Chicago,*[1] *District of Columbia v. Heller,*[2] *New York State Rifle & Pistol Assn., Inc. v. Bruen,*[3] and *United States v. Rahimi.*[4] In brief, the Court in *Heller* and *McDonald* recognized that the Second and Fourteenth Amendments protect the right of an ordinary, law-abiding citizen to possess a handgun *in the home for self-defense.* In *Bruen,* the court further held that ordinary, law-abiding citizens have a similar right to carry handguns *publicly* for their self-defense. Thus, "the Second and Fourteenth Amendments protect an individual's right to carry a handgun for self-defense *outside the home.*"[5] Importantly, *Bruen* held that it is *unconstitutional* to require an applicant for a public carry license to demonstrate a *"special need"* or an *"urgent need"* for self-defense. As a result, no state may prevent law-abiding citizens from publicly carrying handguns because they have not demonstrated a "special need for self-defense."

At the time of the *Bruen* decision, the Court noted that 43 states are "shall issue" jurisdictions, where authorities must issue concealed-carry licenses whenever applicants satisfy certain threshold requirements, without granting licensing officials discretion to deny licenses based on a perceived lack of need or suitability. But in six jurisdictions, additional conditions are required before a license to carry is issued; a citizen must also demonstrate some *special or urgent need.* Those jurisdictions include California, the District of Columbia, Hawaii, Maryland, Massachusetts, New Jersey, and New York. These jurisdictions require the applicant to "demonstrate a special need for self-protection distinguishable from that of the general community." Consequently, these jurisdictions, and others, have been revisiting their laws in this regard.

Currently, Florida is a "Permitless Carry" (also known as "Constitutional Carry") state (explained in greater detail in Chapter 7). In short, if you are legally allowed to own a firearm, you don't need a permit to carry it. However, it is strongly recommended to take a

---

[1] *McDonald v. Chicago*, 561 U. S. 742, 778, 130 S.Ct. 3020 (2010).

[2] *District of Columbia v. Heller*, 554 U. S. 570, 128 S.Ct. 2783 (2008).

[3] *New York State Rifle & Pistol Assn., Inc. v. Bruen*, 597 U. S. 1, 17, 142 S.Ct. 2111 (2022).

[4] *United States v. Rahimi*, 602 U.S. 680, 144 S.Ct. 1889 (2024).

[5] *New York State Rifle & Pistol Assn., Inc. v. Bruen*, 597 U. S. 1, 8-10, 142 S.Ct. 2122 (2022).

concealed carry course and earn certification for several important reasons:

- The law could change at any time.
- You will gain essential knowledge.
- You will pass a basic proficiency test.
- You will receive a Florida Concealed Carry License.
- Having a license waives the waiting period for purchasing a new handgun.

A benefit of permitless carry is that if your license lapses (maybe due to moving and missing the renewal paperwork), you can still carry legally. I know of one individual who faced this situation, and he opted to retake the course. It was an entirely different experience from his first. The initial instructor was NRA-certified, while the second instructor had a background in law enforcement.

It is hard to say which course was better, but even if you are having second thoughts after completing the course, concealed carry might still be right for you, provided you have strong firearm proficiency. If you're still getting your skills up, that's ok. Taking honest self-assessments is healthy. You can continue alone with the permit process, and your instructor can give you a mock qualification to determine if you're ready.

A responsible person will always think of what could go wrong and may second-guess themselves, while an overconfident person might ignore the lessons or skip getting a permit altogether. If you're reading this book, you're likely in the former group, and I commend you for it. This text is designed to give you the knowledge and confidence you need to carry responsibly and understand various scenarios.

Finally, this book will cover everything from different holsters and carry methods to real-world situations, ensuring you're a well-informed, responsible, and law-abiding armed citizen. Additionally, there will be a discussion on the importance of insurance for those who carry handguns. If you're already constitutionally carrying, this is vital. Should you ever find yourself in a situation with legal implications, you will want to ensure both you and your finances are protected.

Notes

USCCA Gun Safety Rules, see https://www.iftnra.com/firearms-safety-rules.

Chapter Two
Gun Safety

Section

§ 2.1. Preliminary

- Respect any gun as if it were loaded.
- Finger off the trigger.
- Always point in a safe direction.
- Use extreme caution when inserting firearms into holsters, and only use high-quality holsters designed for your specific model.
- Train yourself to a proficiency you can maintain.
- Inspect firearms or hand them off with the action open.
- Seek out workshops or well-respected instructors you can learn from.

Always exercise caution when handling a firearm. When you purchase a new gun, it's important to learn how to properly field strip, clean, and lubricate your weapon. Choosing high-quality ammunition is also important for your safety. Reloaded ammunition may be less expensive, but it could damage your firearm, or even worse, you could be injured.

§ 2.2. Firearms without a safety

With firearms that don't have a safety, it is vital that you don't modify the trigger pull. While switching to a flat trigger may be ok if it's from an authorized manufacturer, replacing the springs in your gun for a reduction in the trigger pull could be dangerous and make your pistol unreliable. If you are carrying a gun without a safety, it could be especially dangerous.

For firearms that don't have a manual safety lever, the responsibility for safety falls directly on you, and the trigger becomes your primary safeguard. This means that as long as your finger remains off the trigger, the firearm will not discharge. Proper trigger discipline is critical; never place your finger on the trigger until you are ready to shoot. Always use high-quality holsters designed specifically for your gun model and submodel.

Understanding this concept is essential for safe firearm handling, especially with modern concealed carry pistols. These are often designed without a manual safety for quicker and more efficient draw times. These firearms are built to be secure so long as they are handled correctly, meaning they won't accidentally fire unless the trigger is intentionally pulled.

Maintaining control over the firearm and always keeping your finger outside the trigger guard until you're ready to engage a target are non-negotiable habits. Remember, you are the ultimate safety feature of any firearm. Practicing proper handling and trigger discipline ensures that you can carry with confidence, knowing that you are in control at all times.

Find a gun that has a trigger pull you are comfortable with before you purchase it. If you are using a revolver, practicing de-cocking with your gun unloaded is an important fundamental.

In the Matter of Moises M.

Central Falls, R.I. (Oct. 24, 2024)

Moises M., the suspect accused in a fatal shooting of a 14-year-old girl on Earl Street in Central Falls, told police that the gun he was handling accidentally went off when it struck the victim and later killed her.

Mr. M. (18 years old) told investigators he woke up in the bedroom of the victim's boyfriend's home on Earle Street, and received a text from the victim "asking to purchase marijuana pods." He said he and the victim met up and he laid out different flavors of the pods on the bed, where the victim sat.

Mr. M. admitted to investigators that on the morning of the incident, he was also handling a Glock he claimed belonged to a friend. He said he picked it up and began to clear the gun of ammunition when "it accidentally discharged," striking the victim.

Panicking, Mr. M. informed others in the house, who advised him to leave. Mr. M. now faces a manslaughter charge after the 14-year-old girl died from the gunshot wound, as well as a charge of possession of a firearm without a license.

Shooting on the "Rust" Movie Set

Bonanza Creek Ranch, Santa Fe, New Mexico

The need for firearm safety was spotlighted on October 21, 2021, by the fatal shooting on the set of the movie "Rust," which occurred when, in the course of rehearsing a scene, a prop revolver held by Alec Baldwin accidentally discharged a live round, killing cinematographer Halyna Hutchins and injuring director Joel Souza.

At the time, Baldwin was rehearsing a scene in a church when the gun went off. Baldwin said he didn't pull the trigger and that he was told the gun was safe before it was handed to him. However, an FBI forensic report found that the gun, a .45 caliber Colt revolver, could not fire without the trigger being pulled. Baldwin then argued that there was never supposed to be a real bullet on set at all.

Although props departments may use real guns on movie sets, as a rule, they do not use live ammunition. Typically, they use blanks to re-create the effect of firing a gun, sometimes with added powder for better "blasts." Despite those general firearm-safety practices, the gun Baldwin was using turned out to have a "live" round inside.

As a result of the shooting, first assistant director David Halls, who handed the Colt .45 revolver to Baldwin, was convicted of the negligent use of a deadly weapon. Halls was sentenced to six months of unsupervised probation as part of a plea deal.

Prosecutors charged Baldwin and the movie's prop armorer, Hannah Gutierrez-Reed, with two counts each of involuntary manslaughter. In late April 2023, they dropped the charges against Baldwin, but Gutierrez-Reed stood trial, was found guilty of manslaughter in April 2024, and was sentenced to 18 months in prison.

(Continued on the next page)

In January 2023, prosecutors empaneled another grand jury that again indicted Baldwin on the involuntary manslaughter charge. Prosecutors cited a new report that contradicted Baldwin's claim that he had never fired the gun. Baldwin once again pleaded not guilty, and his trial began on July 9, 2024.

On July 12, 2024, the involuntary manslaughter case against Alec Baldwin was dismissed by Judge Mary Marlowe Sommer. The judge ruled that prosecutors intentionally withheld evidence from the defense, including a batch of bullets that could have been connected to the shooting.

Clearly, if any one of these three people—Alec Baldwin, Hannah Gutierrez-Reed, or David Halls—had practiced firearm safety protocol, Halyna Hutchins would be alive today. According to one prosecutor, the "evidence clearly shows a pattern of criminal disregard for safety on the Rust film set."

Bonanza Creek Ranch used for the set of the Movie "Rust," Sante Fe, N.M. Jae C. Hong/AP, FILE.

Notes

CHAPTER THREE
CARRY STYLES, TECHNIQUES & METHODS

Section

§ 3.1. Preliminary

Once you begin carrying—whether open or concealed—it's going to feel very foreign to you. When carrying concealed, you will wonder if people around you know; you may keep checking your clothing in the area or move differently. It's important that instead of thinking you're being watched, you try to act naturally. It is also important to note that when open carrying a handgun, *you must keep the handgun holstered.*

Sig Sauer P10 Cocked and Locked IWB; This holster has a snap that holds the hammer back in conjunction with the gun's safety, providing an extra layer of protection.

§ 3.2. Printing

Printing is the term used when the pattern of a gun can be seen under your clothes. You want to avoid this by dressing around your gun. If you typically wear slim or tight jeans, you may want to switch to a different cut or go up a size. If you're not comfortable, it's not repeatable, meaning over time you will slowly stop carrying altogether. This is a commitment that you're making. Carrying a concealed weapon should be as simple as having your wallet, car keys, cell phone, and your carry rig. Your "everyday carry" ("EDC") should be as comfortable as putting on your shoes.

§ 3.3. Other acronyms

Sig Sauer P365 in Vedder Kydex holster with adjustable cant and wing.

In addition to "EDC" ("everyday carry"), other acronyms include "IWB" ("inside the waistband") and "OWB" ("outside the waistband").

You can carry on your person or in a bag. If you choose to carry in a bag, it should be a specialized one designed to carry a firearm.

§ 3.4. Holsters and bags

Whatever system you use, it must have a holster that completely covers the trigger.

- IWB
- OWB
- Fanny Pack
- Concealed Carry Purse
- Ankle Holster
- Pocket Holster
- Shoulder Holster
- Tactical Sling/Leg Bag
- Thigh holster
- Belly band
- Waistband holster

Learning which method or combination works best for you takes time and is an additional investment. Anyone you know who's been carrying concealed for years will have a drawer or box full of holsters!

A recommendation for IWB is the "wing" as shown on the holster on the previous page. It tilts the firearm grip back towards your body instead of printing through your shirt. Presently, there are no restrictions placed on the type of holster, so you may use belly bands, waistband holsters, pocket holsters, ankle holsters, thigh holsters, etc.

A concealed-carry bag is a purpose-built bag. These gun bags are not commonly sold in gun stores or at shows, but can be found online. This bag by Vi Vante has zippers on each side making it ambidextrous. If the owner feels threatened, they can actually have their hand inside the bag and on their gun. If need be, the gun can be fired through the bag without pulling it out.

This Vi Vante Zenith Shadow Pro Tactical Leg Bag may be found at: https://vi-vante.com.

We The People Car Gun Mount - Dual Locking & Universal Flat Mounting Car Holster, as shown at Amazon.com

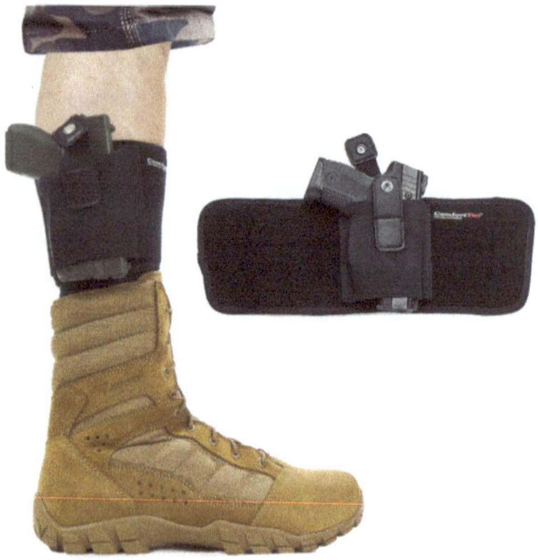

ComfortTac Ankle Holster, compatible with Glock 42, 43, 36, 26, S&W Bodyguard .30, .38, Ruger LCP, LC9, Sig Sauer and similar guns.

Nylon Shoulder Holster found at craftholsters.com.

Chapter Four
Choosing A Firearm

Section
§ 4.1. Caliber and ammunition
§ 4.2. Concealment capabilities
§ 4.3. Securing your firearms

§ 4.1. Caliber and ammunition

Making the right choice for you, concealed carry doesn't have to be a difficult one. First, determine the size of the pistol you want to carry. For deep concealment, *e.g.,* IWB (inside the waistband, with holster), you will want the most reliable compact gun you can shoot well. A few examples follow. Remember, these are just examples; you have to choose what fits best into your lifestyle:

- Sig Sauer P238, P938, 365
- Springfield Armory XD, Hellcat
- Ruger LCP, LCR
- S&W Shield Plus
- Beretta PX4 Storm CC 2
- Colt Python 3-inch
- Glock 43
- S&W Bodyguard
- Walther PDP-F 3.5-Inch
- Walther PPK 380

Should you need to choose a firearm for open carry versus concealed carry, there isn't a one-size-fits-all solution. There is a range of firearms that can cross over for both tasks, such as the Sig Sauer P365 and Springfield Hellcat lines. They offer a variety of sizes, making them a great choice for either job. For open carry, we recommend the HK P30S, VP9, Sig Sauer M11-A1, P226, Springfield 1911 Prodigy 9mm DS (double stack, high capacity), and Smith & Wesson 686. We do not recommend the P320 for safety reasons (accidental discharges have been reported).

The most common rounds for this task are .380 and 9mm. A 380 is half of a 9mm round. That doesn't mean half the stopping power.

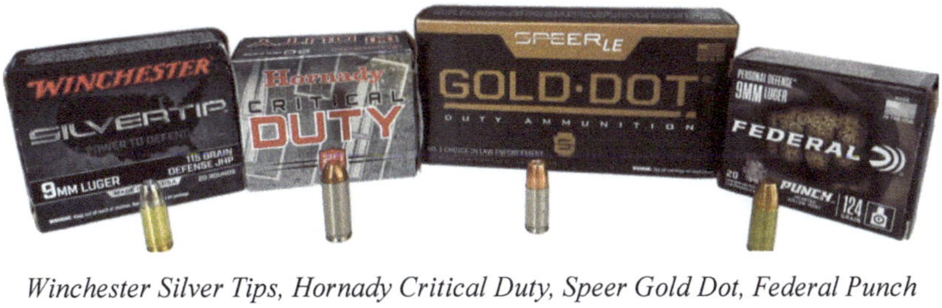

Winchester Silver Tips, Hornady Critical Duty, Speer Gold Dot, Federal Punch

It is essential to use hollow points or defensive rounds rather than FMJ (full metal jacket). Defensive rounds create a larger wound track in an assailant, and if you miss, they over-penetrate. A critical point in defensive shooting situations is to *always* immediately analyze beyond the threat and consider possible outcomes. Note, however, that not all states are as friendly as Florida for such ammunition. Certain states, such as New Jersey, prohibit the use of hollow points or dum-dum bullets.

.380 on the Left and 9mm on the right after being fired into a ballistics gel

The ballistics of the 9mm and .380 ACP (Automatic Colt Pistol) are closer than you may think. The .380 ACP will have less penetration, but the round will have similar effects to a 9mm on an assailant. In a compact handgun for someone with less strength, a .380 ACP is an excellent choice because of the reduction in recoil.

Optics are a fabulous addition to concealed carry; they give you the ability to acquire a target with both eyes open while maintaining situational awareness. The advantage of using optics on your handgun is that you will be more proficient than with your non-optic iron sights. Note, however, that it should be expected that when you use a piece of technology, it can fail you at some point. Batteries, cheap ammo, and poor cleaning habits are some of the potential weak links in a chain of variables.

§ 4.2. Concealment capabilities

The concealed firearm market has evolved dramatically over the past few years, offering a stunning range of options. For example, the smallest versions of the Sig Sauer P365 or Springfield Hellcat are compact models that also feature magazines with pinky extensions for a more secure grip, a design touch reminiscent of the classic PPK. When selecting the right firearm for concealment, it's wise to consider not only the size and weight but also the magazine options and capacity. Staying with factory parts is essential, as they are designed to meet rigorous safety standards, adding an extra layer of reliability to your setup.

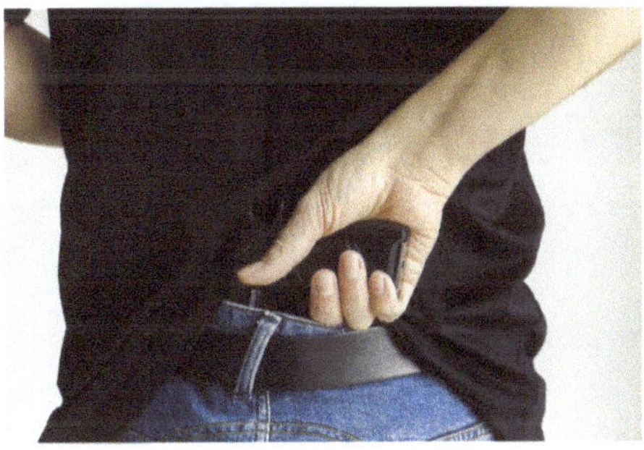

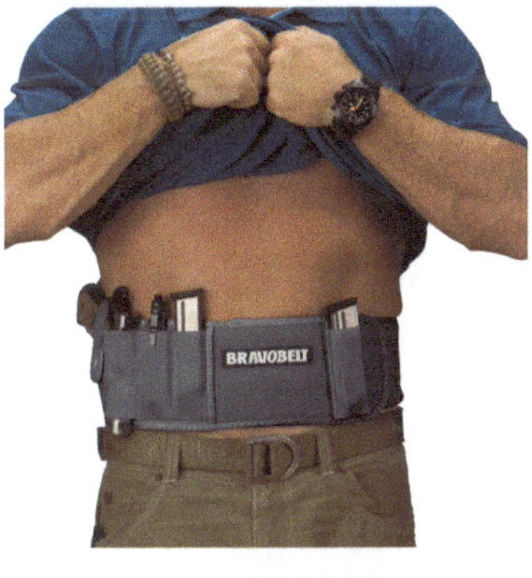

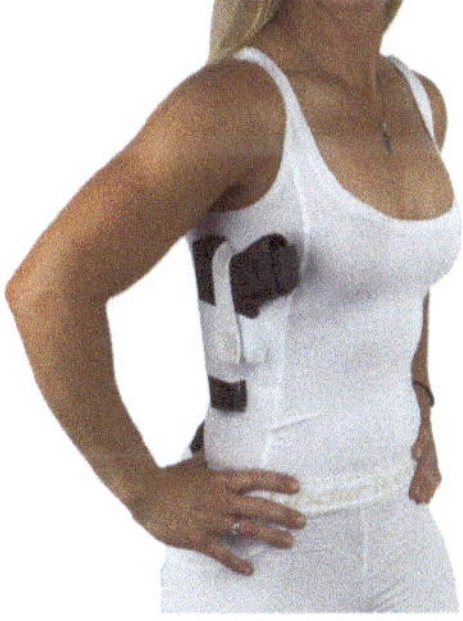

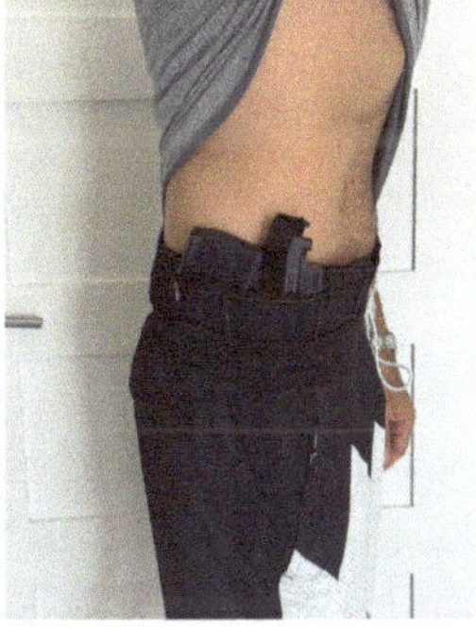

§ 4.3. Securing your firearms

Keeping your firearms secure is paramount with gun safety, and you *must* take extra care if there are children who could get access to one of them. Indeed, many states have laws with severe penalties for leaving an easily accessible firearm within reach of a child.[6]

Make sure that when you're not home, no guns are left out anywhere that can be easily accessed. Consider investing in a gun safe, such as a night table rapid safe, or even a clock or book safe. The goal is to avoid any of the following individuals from getting unauthorized access:

- Children
- Roommates
- House guests
- Contractors
- Housekeepers
- Burglars/Robbers/Uninvited intruders

---

[6] *See, e.g.,* 784.05(3), Florida Stat., which provides that a person exposes another to personal injury through culpable negligence "by storing or leaving a loaded firearm within the reach or easy access of a minor commits, if the minor obtains the firearm and uses it to inflict injury or death upon himself or herself or any other person, a ***felony of the third degree***[.]" This section does not apply, however: "(a) if the firearm was stored or left in a securely locked box or container or in a location which a reasonable person would have believed to be secure, or was securely locked with a trigger lock; (b) If the minor obtains the firearm as a result of an unlawful entry by any person . . .").

See also 790.174, Florida Stat. ("(1) A person who stores or leaves, on a premise under his or her control, a loaded firearm, . . . , and who knows or reasonably should know that a minor is likely to gain access to the firearm without the lawful permission of the minor's parent or the person having charge of the minor, or without the supervision required by law, shall keep the firearm in a securely locked box or container or in a location which a reasonable person would believe to be secure or shall secure it with a trigger lock, except when the person is carrying the firearm on his or her body or within such close proximity thereto that he or she can retrieve and use it as easily and quickly as if he or she carried it on his or her body." A violation may be a ***misdemeanor of the second degree.***

Gun safety is not just a responsibility; it's a commitment. As a firearm owner, you must always ensure that your gun is handled, stored, and maintained safely. This responsibility doesn't end when you're done carrying for the day; it extends to how and where you store your firearm, making sure no one else can access it, especially children, guests, or unauthorized individuals.

There are also numerous concealment products available on the market. Here, you can be creative and secretive at the same time. These are available at Amazon.com:

Notes

CHAPTER FIVE
TRAINING

Section

§ 5.1. Preliminary

Even if you have extensive shooting experience, it is extremely important to approach this subject with an open mind, a willingness to learn, and no ego. Countless times, the authors go to the gun range only to see people barely hit the target in a completely controlled situation. It's a complete waste of ammunition. The money spent on shots that miss the target would be better spent on an instructor who can teach how to hone your skills to make better groupings.

Proper instruction can help you establish a baseline for a more effective use of your firearm. Just think, if you ever find yourself in a crisis and your gun is the only thing between you and an armed assailant, you need to be able to neutralize the threat. It's through consistent training that using your firearm can become second nature. A good instructor can also simulate gun jams, stress, and quick judgments.

§ 5.2. Private instruction vs. group classes/workshops

This is a personal choice. We strongly recommend that, as soon as you make the decision to start your concealed carry journey, you invest in private training. This one-on-one instruction will help you build a solid foundation, reinforcing essential gun safety practices and preventing bad habits from forming right from the start. Think of it as setting the groundwork for everything that follows. Private training ensures you're learning the correct techniques, which will make your solo practice sessions more effective and beneficial.

Once you have established a strong foundation, consider expanding your skills by participating in group classes. These sessions often focus on specific topics within the realm of concealed carry, such as defensive shooting, drawing from concealment, or situational awareness. Group classes also provide a great opportunity to learn from others and gain experience in various scenarios. For example, at places like Okeechobee Shooting Sports, you'll find a designated area specifically for practicing drawing from concealment, an essential skill for anyone serious about carrying.

No matter which path you choose, the key is to train consistently. Regular practice not only helps you maintain your skills but also allows you to continue learning, refining, and improving your abilities. Concealed carry is a journey, and ongoing training is what keeps you sharp, confident, and ready for whatever situation may arise.

By purchasing this book, you've already taken an important step in the right direction, and we commend you for your commitment to responsible firearm ownership. Now, keep that momentum going by investing in the training you need to be safe, proficient, and prepared.

§ 5.3. Range safety and protocol

Consider the capabilities of the particular gun range you choose to use. Be sure to bring a pistol case so you don't violate range rules. Also, when planning to visit a gun range, call the range or check its website to see if there is a dress code. Some ranges and shooting clubs have specific dress code requirements.

At the range, wear clothing that protects you from the elements and provides firearm safety, such as:

- A hat: A hat protects your head and face from ejected cartridges and keeps hair out of your eyes.
- A shirt with a collar prevents spent casings from falling down your clothes. Avoid low-cut shirts, tank tops, or see-through or cropped shirts.
- Long pants are recommended, especially if you plan to shoot from a prone position. The more skin you have covered at the range means the less likely you are to go home with a burn. It's also a good idea to wear comfortable, loose-fitting pants to make it easier to move while shooting or practicing your stance. Tactical or cargo pants are lightweight, breathable, and built to last; they have plenty of pockets to store extra mags, etc.
- Shoes: Wear comfortable, closed-toed shoes. Do NOT wear open-toed shoes, sandals, flip-flops, ballet flats, or high heels. Hot brass from ejected cartridges can burn your feet and toes.

- DO NOT wear a lot of jewelry. Large, dangling earrings, bracelets, etc., could interfere with your shooting.

- Hoods and facial coverings should not be worn inside the range; your attire should not block your identifying features.

- Always wear eye and ear protection when shooting, and when in the area where others may be shooting.

Before and during arrival at the range:

- Treat all firearms as loaded: Always treat every firearm as if it were loaded, even if you're told that it is unloaded.

- Upon arrival, all guns and rifles must be unloaded and safely secured in a case or bag. Range staff will check your ammunition every time. Keep firearms and ammunition separate, and load or unload only on the firing line.

- Check the range rules regarding holsters; many indoor ranges prohibit drawing from holsters. Also, most ranges prohibit the use of reloaded or remanufactured ammunition, as well as strictly prohibiting the use of tracer, incendiary, explosive, or armor-piercing ammunition.

- CAUTION: Lead is toxic; there is no eating or drinking on the range, and obviously no smoking. When you are done shooting, be sure to thoroughly wash your hands and use a special soap, such as Hygenall LeadOff or ESCA-Tech D-Lead Hand Soap. Pregnant women should not be in the range. LEAD IS IRREVERSIBLY HAZARDOUS TO A FETUS!

- Know your firearm: Familiarize yourself with your firearm before firing it. Know how to load and unload it, engage the safety mechanism, and clear any malfunctions.

- When you are about to begin, *bring your weapon to the firing line in a gun bag.* Do not take the weapon out and risk pointing it around the room while you make your way to the firing line.

Vi Vante "Elite Luxe" soft pistol case, gun range bag, availabale at Amazon.com

- Keep the muzzle of the firearm pointed downrange at all times. This ensures that stray bullets are less likely to hit people in the event of an accident. It is important to always keep the gun pointed in a safe direction; loaded or not, maintain muzzle awareness.
- Be sure of your target: Be aware of what's in your line of fire, including your target, backstop, and beyond.
- Fire from the designated firing line; most ranges have a designated firing line where you should shoot. Only fire at targets intended for that position.

It is important to remember that the gun range managers have the final say in determining appropriate safe gun handling, proper ammunition, rate of fire, appropriate behavior, appropriate dress, or whether there is a suspicion of someone being under the influence of drugs and/or alcohol. Failure to comply with an ejection order will most likely result in a call to the police.

Don't forget to carefully scan the area before leaving. All too often, range goers forget something important and only realize what is missing upon arriving home.

§ 5.4. Dry firing

Dry fire training involves everything you can do with a weapon without actually firing any rounds. While it should not replace live firing, it is a highly recommended element of any firearms training regimen as it provides a safe way to hone your shooting skills at home, without the need to schedule range time or incur range and ammunition costs. Allowing mastery of basics like grip, stance, sight alignment, and trigger control outside of the range, dry fire training has evolved significantly over the years. A well-known technique for enhancing trigger control has been the coin drill, where a coin is placed on the barrel of an unloaded firearm, and the aim is to pull the trigger without dislodging the coin. With advancements in technology, new sophisticated systems have emerged. One highly recommended system is the *Strikeman* system (http://www.strikeman.io), which utilizes your cell phone to monitor your accuracy. Whether you use the coin, an advanced technological system, or a combination of both, dry fire training will help you enhance your shooting skills. Remember, even with dry fire exercises, always handle your firearm as if it's loaded and ensure it is pointed safely.

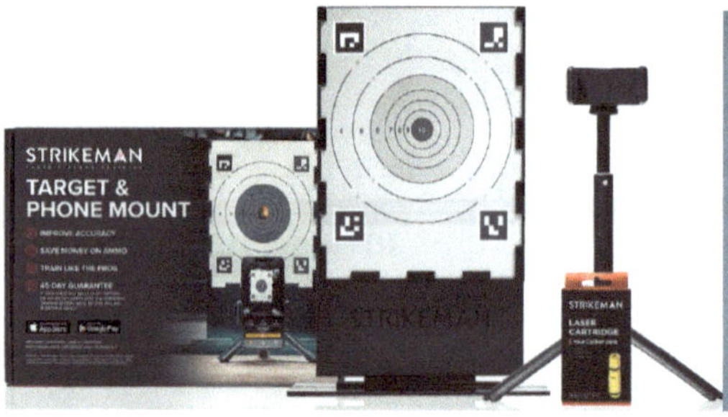

---

§ 5.5. Training recommendations

- Become an ambidextrous shooter.
- Practice at different distances.
- Go to different gun ranges indoors and outdoors to get used to shooting in different environments and conditions.

- Don't always use the same targets; classic silhouettes are great, but bull's eyes are better. Using targets that have multiple bullseyes is a great way to move from target to target. Change it up each time you train.

- Use the right protective equipment that gives you an edge. Clearer glasses like Wiley X can help you see better, and active ear protection can save your hearing.
- Use high-quality range ammo. Occasionally, it's a good idea to use your defensive rounds and replace your magazine in your carry with fresh ones every few months. If you're shooting 9mm, that's 115 grain.[7] You can mix in some 124-grain to simulate the feeling of shooting +P defensive rounds, too.

---

§ 5.6. Apply for a concealed weapon license

Once you've completed your required training, the next step is to apply for your Florida Concealed Carry License. There are a few ways to make this process as smooth and efficient as possible:

[7] "115 Grain" is a unit of weight used to measure the weight of the actual bullet. It is equal to 1/7000th of a pound.

1. In-Person at the Tax Collector's Office or the Department of Agriculture

The quickest and most direct way to apply is by visiting your local Tax Collector's Office or a regional office of the Florida Department of Agriculture and Consumer Services (FDACS). At these locations, you can complete your application, submit your fingerprints, and have your photo taken, all in one visit. This method can significantly expedite the processing time compared to other options. For more information and to find the nearest locations, visit the official FDACS website:

https://www.fdacs.gov/Consumer-Resources/Concealed-Weapon-License/Applying-for-a-Concealed-Weapon-License#inperson

2. Applying by Mail. If you prefer, you can also apply for your license by mail. Here's how:

- Have your fingerprints taken at your local police station or an authorized fingerprinting service. Make sure they use the standard fingerprint card approved by the state.
- Download the concealed carry application from the FDACS website and fill it out completely.
- Submit the completed application, your fingerprint card, and a check or money order for the appropriate fee to the address provided on the application form.

While applying by mail can be convenient, it may take longer to process than applying in person. Be sure to double-check that all your documents are properly filled out and that you've included the correct payment amount to avoid any delays.

Tip: No matter which method you choose, it's a good idea to keep copies of all the documents you submit and note the date of your application. This can help if you need to follow up on the status of your license. Do it right the first time and prevent delays.

CHAPTER SIX
USE OF FORCE

Section

§ 6.1. Florida's "Stand Your Ground" law

Florida's "Stand Your Ground" law relieves citizens of the duty to retreat in the face of imminent violence or the commission of a violent crime. Florida is not the only state that permits people to defend themselves against a threat in places they are lawfully permitted to be—28 other states and Puerto Rico have similar laws on their books.

A revision to Florida's law in 2005 removed the obligation of someone to retreat before fighting back, a broader level of permission for justifiable force than other states have, which means if you are lawfully permitted to be on premises other than your own private property (house, lawn, etc.), and you're threatened, then you have the right to defend yourself up to and including using deadly force.

For example, if you are in line at a convenience store and an armed assailant comes in, threatening you and asking for money in the cash register, you may fight back with your own weapon to prevent the commission of that felony.

Florida's stand your ground law also provides you with immunity from prosecution if you are within the bounds of self-defense or justifiable homicide.[8] In *Love v. State*, the Florida Supreme Court further explained:

---

[8] *See, e.g., Lovett v. State*, 30 Fla. 142, 163-64 (Fla. 1892) (permitting a homicide to be excused if the person who committed it reasonably believed there was no other way to prevent bodily harm). Note that the "conduct of a person acting in self-defense is measured by an objective standard, but the standard must be applied to the facts and circumstances as they appeared at the time of the altercation to the one acting in self-defense." *Shreiteh v. State*, 987 So. 2d 761, 763 (Fla. 4th DCA 2008); *see also Chaffin v. State*, 121 So. 3d 608, 612 (Fla. 4th DCA 2013) ("The law does not ascribe a subjective standard as to a defendant's state of mind but concerns a reasonably prudent person's state of mind.").

Under the *Stand Your Ground* law, a person is generally "immune from criminal prosecution and civil action" when that person justifiably uses or threatens to use force under certain circumstances. FLA. STAT. § 776.032(1). The criminal immunity "includes arresting, detaining in custody, and charging or prosecuting the defendant." FLA. STAT. § 776.032(1).[9]

It should be noted, however, that the Stand Your Ground law *does not confer civil liability immunity* to a criminal defendant based upon an immunity determination in the criminal case."[10] Here's the law:

§ 776.012. Use or threatened use of force in defense of person.

(1) A person is justified in using or threatening to use force, except deadly force, against another when and to the extent that the person reasonably believes that such conduct is necessary to defend himself or herself or another against the other's imminent use of unlawful force. A person who uses or threatens to use force in accordance with this subsection ***does not have a duty to retreat*** before using or threatening to use such force.

(2) A person is justified in using or threatening to use deadly force if he or she reasonably believes that using or threatening to use such force is necessary to prevent imminent death or great bodily harm to himself or herself or another or to prevent the imminent commission of a forcible felony. ***A person who uses or threatens to use deadly force in accordance with this subsection does not have a duty to retreat and has the right to stand his or her ground*** if the person using or threatening to use the deadly force is not engaged in a criminal activity and is in a place where he or she has a right to be.

Rev. § 2, ch. 2005-27; § 3, ch. 2014-195.

---

[9] *Love v. State*, 286 So.3d 177, 180 (2019); *see also Boston v. State,* 326 So.3d 673 (2021) (Regarding the burden of proof in a "stand your ground" case, § 776.032 was amended in 2017 to provide: "(4) In a criminal prosecution, once a *prima facie* claim of self-defense immunity from criminal prosecution has been raised by the defendant at a pretrial immunity hearing, the burden of proof by clear and convincing evidence is on the party seeking to overcome the immunity from criminal prosecution provided in subsection (1)."). "In light of the 2017 amendment, a defendant is no longer required to prove that he or she acted in self-defense by a preponderance of the evidence at an immunity hearing; instead, a defendant need only make a *prima facie* showing at that point. To defeat the claim of immunity, the State must prove by clear and convincing evidence that the defendant did not act in self-defense." *Boston* at 675.

[10] *Kumar v. Patel*, 227 So.3d 557, 558 (2017).

"Stand Your Ground" Elements:

(1) You may use or threaten deadly force *and*
(2) You DO NOT have a duty to retreat; you may "stand your ground,"
(3) When you reasonably believe it is necessary
(4) To prevent imminent death or great bodily harm:
(5) (a) To yourself or another; *or*
 (b) To prevent the imminent commission of a forcible felony.

Two Conditions:

(1) You must not be engaged in criminal activity; and
(2) You must be in a place where you have a right to be.

Martin v. State

414 So.3d 195 (4th DCA 2025)

"The State charged Martin with battery on a person over 65 years of age. Martin filed a motion to dismiss seeking immunity under Florida's Stand Your Ground law, section 776.032, Florida Stat., based upon a claim that he acted in self-defense."

The victim in this case was working as a valet driver with Martin on the day of the incident. The victim's roles were to hand out valet tickets and park vehicles. After the victim parked a vehicle, Martin cursed at him and stated he was missing valet tickets. The two men argued over the tickets. The victim acknowledged that he raised his voice and "got close" to Martin during the exchange. At some point during the argument, Martin punched the victim. The victim claimed Martin did not try to walk away from him during the altercation. However, video footage of the incident shows Martin walking away from the alleged victim prior to the punch at issue.

An eyewitness at the scene stated that she had observed the victim yelling at Martin, and Martin trying to calm the victim down. From about thirty feet away, the eyewitness observed the victim pointing his finger in Martin's face. After the victim "got very close" to Martin, Martin punched him. The eyewitness then observed the victim following Martin while cursing at him.

(Continued on the next page)

According to Martin, *who has only one arm,* on the day of the incident, the victim showed up late to the valet station and had an angry demeanor. Because the victim was struggling to operate newer vehicles, the two switched roles. However, even in the role switch, the victim was handling the tickets improperly. When Martin tried to explain things to the victim, he got upset as if Martin was trying to "boss him around." During the exchange, the victim got very close to Martin and then threatened him while poking Martin in the chest a couple of times, and showed Martin pictures of him on his phone from his "bodybuilding days."

According to Martin, he attempted to walk away from the victim three times during the entirety of the altercation, and the video footage reflects the third time he attempted to do so. During Martin's third attempt to walk away, the victim grabbed Martin's shirt. At that point, Martin believed the alleged victim wanted to harm him. Although Martin tried to walk away, the alleged victim "kept on trying to get in [Martin's] face and trying to touch [Martin]." *Id.* at 196-97.

In this appeal, given the circumstances facing Martin, the court held that the force used "was justified and proportional to the event. These circumstances included: (1) Martin having only one arm; (2) the alleged victim's verbal threats during the heated exchange; (3) the alleged victim's act of 'getting close' to Martin and raising his voice (by his own admission); (4) Martin's testimony that he believed the alleged victim wanted to harm him; and (5) the alleged victim's act of pointing his finger in Martin's face and grabbing Martin's shirt as Martin attempted to walk away for a third time." *Id.* at 198.

"Simply put, based on the circumstances as they appeared to Martin, a reasonable and prudent person situated in the same circumstances and knowing what Martin knew would have used the same force as did Martin." *Id.* (citing *Garcia v. State,* 286 *So.*3d 348, 351 (Fla. 2d DCA 2019) (holding that the objective standard in the Stand Your Ground context requires consideration of "whether, based on the circumstances as they appeared to the defendant, a reasonable and prudent person situated in the same circumstances and knowing what the defendant knew would have used the same force as did the defendant")). Accordingly, Martin's motion to dismiss based on Stand Your Ground immunity should be granted.

Spencer v. State

419 So.3d 654 (4th DCA 2025)

Defendant, charged with second-degree murder following the shooting death of the victim, claims he is immune from prosecution because he reasonably believed that his use of deadly force was necessary to prevent imminent death or great bodily harm or to prevent the imminent commission of a forcible felony.

The shooting occurred at a gated parking lot where the defendant, the victim, and other men worked on cars. Prior to the shooting, the victim had threatened the defendant and had been antagonistic toward other men while at the lot.

On the day of the shooting, the defendant arrived at the parking lot, parked outside, and walked in through the gate. The victim arrived shortly thereafter and demanded that the defendant open the gate so he could pull his car into the lot. The defendant did not open the gate and continued to walk into the lot. The victim began shouting at the defendant and continued to yell at him from his car, repeatedly threatening to "whoop his ass."

When the defendant was about fifty feet into the parking lot, the victim got out of his car and started quickly walking toward the defendant in an aggressive manner. As he neared the defendant, the victim quickened his pace and placed his hands on his front pocket. The defendant saw the victim aggressively approaching him. When the victim was within about six feet of the defendant, the defendant drew his gun from behind his back and fired one shot at the victim.

The victim turned and ran back toward his car. The defendant followed the victim with his gun drawn. As soon as the victim fell to the ground, the defendant unloaded his gun and placed it on the hood of a nearby car. The defendant called 911 less than a minute after the shooting. When the police arrived, they found the victim lying on the ground near his car. Defendant said that he shot the victim because the victim was threatening him. In addition, he told the police that the victim was often antagonistic and had threatened to beat the defendant about two months before the shooting.

(Continued on the next page)

The defendant knew the victim often carried a gun, and he feared he could not defend himself against a physical attack from the victim because the victim was in "great shape," while the defendant had several medical conditions and physical limitations. The defendant also thought the victim might have been carrying his gun because of how he put his hand near his pocket as he approached the defendant. Alternatively, the defendant feared the victim could have taken his gun and used it against him.

In this appeal, the court explained that the legislature created the "Stand Your Ground" law "to immunize persons from criminal prosecution when they are justified in using deadly force. All that is required is that he or she reasonably believe that using such force is necessary to prevent 'imminent death or great bodily harm' or to prevent 'the imminent commission of a forcible felony.'" *Id.* at ___. Relevant considerations include the victim's reputation of being a violent or dangerous person, any prior threats by the victim against the defendant, and the relative physical abilities of the victim and the defendant. *Id.*

No longer does a person have a duty to retreat before using deadly force if he or she "is not engaged in a criminal activity and is in a place where he or she has a right to be." § 776.012(2), Fla. Stat. A defendant need only raise a *prima facie* self-defense claim. . . . Once established, our legislature has declared that the state bears the burden of overcoming a self-defense claim by clear and convincing evidence. § 776.032(4), Fla. Stat. Evidence is clear and convincing when "the truth of the facts asserted is highly probable." . . .

Here, the victim got out of his car and aggressively approached the defendant, yelling at him. The victim had threatened the defendant before and was known to carry a gun. As the victim approached, he moved his hand near his front pocket. Fearing for his life, the defendant drew his gun and shot the victim. "These circumstances support the defendant's position that a reasonable person would have believed that the use of deadly force was necessary to prevent imminent death or great bodily harm or the imminent commission of a forcible felony." *Id.* Thus, the state failed to the meet its burden.

§ 6.2. Use of force and the "21-foot rule"

The "21-foot rule" suggests that someone with a knife running toward you can cover about 21 feet before you could unholster your gun and fire.

The idea's origin dates back to 1982, when Sergeant Dennis Tueller was out on the shooting range with officers practicing drawing and firing their weapons. One new officer asked when he would be justified in shooting someone coming at him with a knife. The officer was essentially asking, "how close is too close?" To experiment, Tueller assigned one officer to play the role of the aggressor. Another was the officer about to be attacked. The attacker would run toward the officer, and they would time how long it would take to reach him. The officers repeated the experiment repeatedly with various role players; men and women, some smaller, others larger.

According to Tueller, the results were "pretty consistent." Said Tueller: "And that was sobering. Because we thought we were doing pretty well, being able to draw and shoot and engage a target at 7 yards in 1½ to 2 seconds. We came to realize that if all you do is stand there and wait for the attacker to come, and you draw and shoot, they can be on top of you before your bullet can take effect." Tueller published an article in SWAT magazine detailing his findings.

Actually, the "21-foot rule" is not an absolute rule, but a flexible guideline based on Tueller's firearms training exercise conducted over four decades ago. Tueller found that "the average healthy adult male," running with a knife or other contact weapon in hand, can cover a distance of seven yards in about 1.5 seconds—the time it takes the "average" officer to draw a sidearm and place two hits center-mass on a man-sized target 21 feet away. Thus, the exercise suggested, within a 21-foot radius, an officer might not have time to draw and successfully defend himself against a charging subject with lethal intent and deadly means before the attacker is on him.

Awareness of this "danger zone" should not be characterized as a "rule," nor should it suggest that any knife-wielder within 21 feet can justifiably be shot.

Fredericks v. State

675 So.2d 989 (1st DCA 1996).

Police responded to a 911 telephone call involving a domestic disturbance in which the defendant allegedly committed a battery against his spouse. Upon arriving at the scene, an incident occurred in which defendant raised a knife, faced one of the officers, and took a step toward him. All three officers present drew their firearms, but the defendant was then abruptly tackled and physically subdued by one of the officers without any shots being fired.

During the trial, the state presented testimony from all three officers concerning their training in confronting a person wielding a knife. The substance of the testimony had to do with the recommended response by an officer when the knife-wielder is at a distance of 21 feet or less from the officer. Because of the danger presented from a possible assailant at this distance, officers are apparently taught to respond with deadly force. The state used this evidence to argue that the officers had a well-founded fear of imminent violence.

Drejka v. State

330 So.3d 1055 (2nd DCA 2021)

During the afternoon, Mr. McGlockton, along with his girlfriend, Brittany, and their three children, stopped at a convenience store to buy snacks. McGlockton improperly parked in a space reserved for persons with disabilities. He exited the car and entered the store with his five-year-old son. Brittany and the couple's younger children waited in the car.

While Mr. McGlockton was in the store, Mr. Drejka drove up, parked adjacent to the disabled parking spot, and began pointing

(Continued on the next page)

at Brittany in a threatening manner. Drejka then stated in an angry and aggressive manner, "People that park here, I give problems to all the time." Eyewitnesses observed Mr. Drejka shouting very loudly and in a threatening manner towards the car. Upon hearing this, Mr. McGlockton left the store. He approached Mr. Drejka and told him to "[g]et away from [his] girl." Mr. McGlockton, who was unarmed, pushed Mr. Drejka to the ground. Mr. McGlockton advanced no further and made no threats. Witnesses say that he turned and retreated several steps, but Drejka drew a gun and shot McGlockton. The bullet pierced McGlockton's heart; he then stumbled back inside the store and died beside his son.

The State called Dr. Roy Bedard, a police trainer, as an expert witness on use of force and defensive tactics. Dr. Bedard explained the "21-foot-rule," a police concept about how fast someone with a knife could close the distance before an officer could draw a gun. "The 21-foot rule provides that a person at a distance of 21 feet or less may pose a threat to the safety of an officer." Specifically, Dr. Bedard related that the 21-foot-rule "doesn't mean that if someone's within 21 feet, you can automatically shoot them." To the contrary, he stressed that invoking the rule is inappropriate when the advancing individual is unarmed.

Buchanan v. City of San Jose

782 Fed. Appx. 589 (No. 17-16100) (9th Cir. 2019)

San Jose police officers shot and killed Phillip Watkins. It is undisputed that Watkins suffered from suicidal despair and arranged to engage the officers in a "suicide by cop" confrontation that resulted in his death.

"The officers responded to an emergency telephone call by Watkins, who falsely reported that there was a man at his address threatening his family with a knife. When the officers arrived at the address, they saw Watkins standing outside the house next to two women, armed with a knife. At that point, the distance between the officers and Watkins was more than 130 feet. It is undisputed that Watkins then immediately advanced toward the officers in a threatening manner[.] Within seconds, both officers opened fire, and Watkins fell to the ground fatally wounded. At the time the officers opened fire, Watkins was approximately 55 feet from them. When Watkins fell, he was approximately 18 feet from the officers."

During the course of its opinion, the court found that the "21-foot rule" cited by the dissent did not enable the plaintiffs to avoid summary judgment. "The 21-foot rule provides that a person at a distance of 21 feet or less from an officer may pose a threat to the officer's safety. Based on this rule, the dissent would hold that there exists a genuine dispute as to whether the officers acted reasonably in this case because Watkins, at a distance of more than 21 feet from the officers, may not have posed an immediate threat to their safety when they began shooting."

"The 21-foot rule provides that a person at a distance of 21 feet or less may pose a threat to the safety of an officer. It does not follow from this rule, or any other, that armed suspects never pose a threat beyond 21 feet. Notably, the dissent does not cite any case holding that an officer must wait until an armed suspect is within 21 feet, or capable of actually inflicting death or serious harm, before being justified in using deadly force."

Accordingly, the "21-foot rule" may provide some insight when determining whether an assailant is too close.

§ 6.3. Castle Doctrine

There is a "centuries-old principle of respect for the privacy of the home,"[11] and it is "beyond dispute that the home is entitled to special protection as the center of the private lives of our people."[12]

As the United States Supreme Court has has noted, "We have, after all, lived our whole national history with an understanding of 'the ancient adage that ***a man's house is his castle*** [to the point that t]he poorest man may in his cottage bid defiance to all the forces of the Crown.'"[13]

As announced by Sir Edward Coke in 1604: Your house is your *"Castle and Fortress."*[14]

Sir Edward Coke

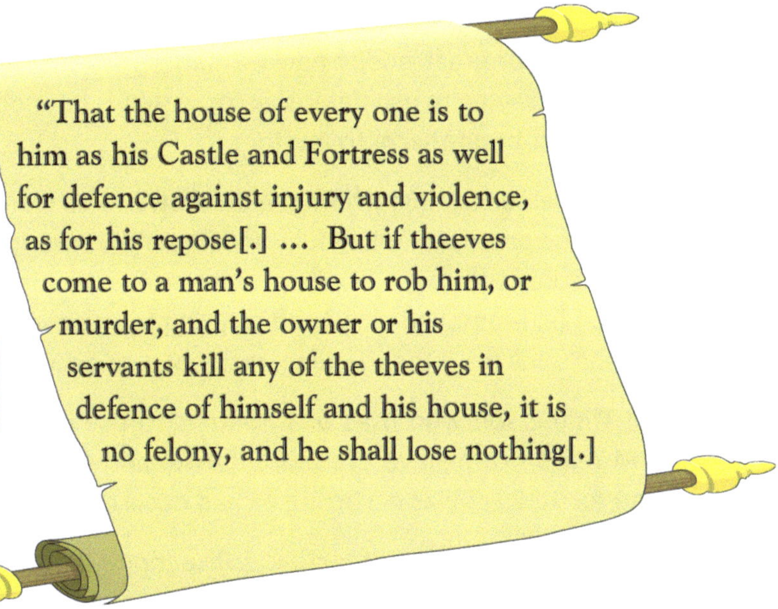

---

[11] *Wilson v. Layne*, 526 U.S. 603, 610, 119 S.Ct. 1692 (1999).

[12] *Minnesota v. Carter*, 525 U.S. 83, 99, 119 S.Ct. 469 (1998) (Kennedy, J., concurring).

[13] *Georgia v. Randolph*, 547 U.S. 103, 115, 126 S.Ct. 1515, 1524 (2006) (quoting *Miller v. United States*, 357 U.S. 301, 307, 78 S.Ct. 1190, 1195 (1958)).

[14] *See also Semayne's Case*, 77 Eng. Rep. 194, 195 (K.B. 1604), 5 Co.Rep. 91a, 91b ("[T]he house of every one is to him as his castle and fortress, as well for his defence against injury and violence as for his repose.").

In pertinent part, Florida statutory law provides:

§ 776.013. Home protection; use or threatened use of deadly force; presumption of fear of death or great bodily harm.

(1) A person who is in a dwelling or residence in which the person has a right to be has no duty to retreat and has the right to stand his or her ground and use or threaten to use:

(a) Nondeadly force against another when and to the extent that the person reasonably believes that such conduct is necessary to defend himself or herself or another against the other's imminent use of unlawful force; or

(b) Deadly force if he or she reasonably believes that using or threatening to use such force is necessary to prevent imminent death or great bodily harm to himself or herself or another or to prevent the imminent commission of a forcible felony.

(2) A person is presumed to have held a reasonable fear of imminent peril of death or great bodily harm to himself or herself or another when using or threatening to use defensive force that is intended or likely to cause death or great bodily harm to another if:

(a) The person against whom the defensive force was used or threatened was in the process of unlawfully and forcefully entering, or had unlawfully and forcibly entered, a dwelling, residence, or occupied vehicle, or if that person had removed or was attempting to remove another against that person's will from the dwelling, residence, or occupied vehicle; and

(b) The person who uses or threatens to use defensive force knew or had reason to believe that an unlawful and forcible entry or unlawful and forcible act was occurring or had occurred.

(3) The presumption set forth in subsection (2) does not apply if:

(a) The person against whom the defensive force is used or threatened has the right to be in or is a lawful resident of the dwelling, residence, or vehicle, such as an owner, lessee, or titleholder, and there is not an injunction for protection from domestic violence or a written pretrial supervision order of no contact against that person; or

(b) The person or persons sought to be removed is a child or grandchild, or is otherwise in the lawful custody or under the lawful guardianship of, the person against whom the defensive force is used or threatened; or

(c) The person who uses or threatens to use defensive force is engaged in a criminal activity or is using the dwelling, residence, or occupied vehicle to further a criminal activity; or

(d) The person against whom the defensive force is used or threatened is a law enforcement officer, as defined in § 943.10(14), who enters or attempts to enter a dwelling, residence, or vehicle in the performance of his or her official duties and the officer identified himself or herself in accordance with any applicable law or the person using or threatening to use force knew or reasonably should have known that the person entering or attempting to enter was a law enforcement officer.

(4) A person who unlawfully and by force enters or attempts to enter a person's dwelling, residence, or occupied vehicle is presumed to be doing so with the intent to commit an unlawful act involving force or violence.

(5) As used in this section, the term: **(a)** ***"Dwelling"*** means a building or conveyance of any kind, including any attached porch, whether the building or conveyance is temporary or permanent, mobile or immobile, which has a roof over it, including a tent, and is designed to be occupied by people lodging therein at night. **(b)** ***"Residence"*** means a dwelling in which a person resides either temporarily or permanently or is visiting as an invited guest. **(c)** ***"Vehicle"*** means a conveyance of any kind, whether or not motorized, which is designed to transport people or property.

§ 1, ch. 2005-27; rev. § 4, ch. 2014-195; § 1, ch. 2017-77.

In A Nutshell

"Castle Doctrine" Elements:

(1) When you are in your own home or lawfully in a residence,
(2) You may use or threaten:
(a) Nondeadly force if you reasonably believe it is necessary to defend against the other's imminent use of unlawful force; *or*
(b) deadly force if you reasonably believe it is necessary to prevent
(i) imminent death or great bodily harm to yourself or another; *or*
(ii) the imminent commission of a forcible felony.
(3) You DO NOT have a duty to retreat; you may "stand your ground."

PRESUMPTIONS:

(1) You are presumed to have a reasonable fear of imminent peril of death or great bodily harm if the intruder was unlawfully and forcefully entering, or had unlawfully and forcibly entered, your *dwelling, residence, or occupied vehicle, OR* if that person had removed or was attempting to remove another against that person's will from the *dwelling, residence, or occupied vehicle.*

(2) You may presume that a person who unlawfully and by force enters or attempts to enter your dwelling, residence, or occupied vehicle is doing so with the intent to commit an unlawful act involving force or violence.

EXCEPTION:

(1) The person against whom the defensive force is used or threatened has the right to be in or is a lawful resident of the dwelling, residence, or vehicle, such as an owner, lessee, or titleholder, and does not have a domestic violence "no contact" order in effect.

(2) You are engaged in criminal activity or is using the dwelling, residence, or occupied vehicle to further a criminal activity.

(3) The person against whom the defensive force is used or threatened is a law enforcement officer acting in the official performance of the officer's duties.

§ 6.4. Using a firearm while under the influence

The use of a firearm by a person while under the influence of an alcoholic beverage, chemical substance, or controlled substance is outlawed by statute, ***so long as your normal faculties are impaired.***

In this regard, the statute reads as follows:

§ 790.151. Using firearm while under the influence.

(1) As used [herein], to "use a firearm" means to discharge a firearm or to have a firearm readily accessible for immediate discharge.

(2) For the purposes of this section, "readily accessible for immediate discharge" means loaded and in a person's hand.

(3) It is unlawful and punishable as provided in subsection (4) for any person who is under the influence of alcoholic beverages, any chemical substance set forth in s. 877.111, or any substance controlled under chapter 893, when affected ***to the extent that his or her normal faculties are impaired,*** to use a firearm in this state.

(4) Any person who violates subsection (3) commits a misdemeanor of the second degree, punishable as provided in s. 775.082 or s. 775.083.

(5) This section does not apply to persons exercising lawful self-defense or defense of one's property.

---

§ 6.5. Immunity

The Florida immunity provisions are set forth below in FLA. STAT. §776.032:

§ 776.032. Immunity[15] from criminal prosecution and civil action for justifiable use or threatened use of force.—

(1) A person who uses or threatens to use force as permitted in § 776.012, § 776.013, or § 776.031 is justified in such conduct and is immune from criminal prosecution and civil action for the use or threatened use of such force by the person, personal representative, or heirs of the person against whom the force was used or threatened, unless the person against whom force was used or threatened is a law enforcement officer, as defined in § 943.10(14), who was acting in the performance of his or her official duties and the officer identified himself or herself in accordance with any

---

[15] *See Peterson v. State*, 983 So.2d 27, 29 (Fla. 1st DCA 2008), where the court upheld the "true immunity" provision in the revised version of Florida's "stand your ground" law. Consequently, persons arrested in connection with an act of "stand your ground" self-defense may avoid prosecution entirely if a judge affirms in the pre-trial hearing that the act was justified, which differs from using castle doctrine or stand your ground as an affirmative defense in a criminal trial. Florida's new laws mean you will not be criminally charged if you are justified in using force. Note also that in 2017, Florida law placed the burden of proof on the prosecution instead of on the defense. Now, in a self-defense pre-trial hearing, the prosecutor must present clear and compelling evidence that the act was not justified under Florida's "stand your ground" criteria.

applicable law or the person using or threatening to use force knew or reasonably should have known that the person was a law enforcement officer. As used in this subsection, the term "criminal prosecution" includes arresting, detaining in custody, and charging or prosecuting the defendant.

(2) A law enforcement agency may use standard procedures for investigating the use or threatened use of force as described in subsection (1), but the agency may not arrest the person for using or threatening to use force unless it determines that there is probable cause that the force that was used or threatened was unlawful.

(3) The court shall award reasonable attorney's fees, court costs, compensation for loss of income, and all expenses incurred by the defendant in defense of any civil action brought by a plaintiff if the court finds that the defendant is immune. . . .

(4) In a criminal prosecution, once a *prima facie* claim of self-defense immunity from criminal prosecution has been raised by the defendant at a pretrial immunity hearing, the burden of proof by clear and convincing evidence is on the party seeking to overcome the immunity from criminal prosecution provided in subsection (1).

Rev. § 6, ch. 2014-195; § 1, ch. 2017-72.

CHAPTER SEVEN
FLORIDA FIREARMS LAWS

The Constitutional Carrying of Concealed Weapons

On July 1, 2023, new legislation had taken effect in the state of Florida which updated a person's authorization to carry a concealed weapon or firearm pursuant to a valid concealed weapons license, ***and added that a person may carry a concealed weapon or firearm without a concealed weapons license*** *(also called "constitutional carry"),* provided that the criteria for obtaining a license is met.

Preemption

Gun laws in Florida are preempted, meaning that counties and local governments cannot enact ordinances that are more restrictive than state laws. This uniformity ensures that gun regulations are consistent throughout the state. An exception may be found in Florida's zoning laws, which may restrict where gun sellers can locate their businesses.

Moreover, Florida has an extreme statutory preemption measure designed to severely restrict local authority to regulate firearms. The measure even includes language intended to personally punish local legislators who cause a preempted law to be passed or enforced.

In this regard, FLA. STAT. § 7900.33(1) provides:

Except as expressly provided by the State Constitution or general law, the Legislature hereby declares that it is occupying the whole field of regulation of firearms and ammunition, including the purchase, sale, transfer, taxation, manufacture, ownership, possession, storage, and transportation thereof, to the exclusion of all existing and future county, city, town, or municipal ordinances or any administrative regulations or rules adopted by local or state government relating thereto. Any such existing ordinances, rules, or regulations are hereby declared null and void.

---

§ 7.1. Pertinent definitions

Pursuant to sections 790.001(3), (4)(a), (9), (10), & (14):

(3) ***"Concealed firearm"*** means any firearm, as defined in subsection (9), which is carried on or about a person in such a manner as to conceal the firearm from the ordinary sight of another person.

(4) (a) ***"Concealed weapon"*** means any dirk, metallic knuckles, billie, tear gas gun, chemical weapon or device, or other deadly weapon carried on or about a person in such a manner as to conceal the weapon from the ordinary sight of another person.

> **NOTE:** A concealed weapon or concealed firearm does not include a machine gun as defined in FLA. STAT. § 790.001(13).

* * * *

(9) ***"Firearm"*** means any weapon (including a starter gun) which will, is designed to, or may readily be converted to expel a projectile by the action of an explosive; the frame or receiver of any such weapon; any firearm muffler or firearm silencer; any destructive device; or any machine gun. The term "firearm" does not include an antique firearm unless the antique firearm is used in the commission of a crime.

(10) ***"Handgun"*** means a firearm capable of being carried and used by one hand, such as a pistol or revolver.

* * * *

(14) ***"Readily accessible for immediate use"*** means that a firearm or other weapon is carried on the person or within such close proximity and in such a manner that it can be retrieved and used as easily and quickly as if carried on the person.

(15) ***"Securely encased"*** means in a glove compartment, whether or not locked; snapped in a holster; in a gun case, whether or not locked; in a zippered gun case; or in a closed box or container which requires a lid or cover to be opened for access.

* * * *

(20) ***"Weapon"*** means any dirk, knife, metallic knuckles, slungshot, billie, tear gas gun, chemical weapon or device, or other deadly weapon except a firearm or a common pocketknife, plastic knife, or blunt-bladed table knife.

Rev. § 1, ch. 2004-286; § 1, ch. 2006-298; § 2, ch. 2016-104; § 4, ch. 2023-18.

"Deadly weapon" is defined by case law to mean a weapon that is "likely to produce death or great bodily injury."[16] Whether or not the weapon involved is to be classed as "deadly" is a factual question to be resolved by the jury or fact finder.[17]

---

[16] *Dale v. State*, 703 So. 2d 1045, 1047 (Fla. 1997).

[17] *Goswick v. State*, 143 So. 2d 817, 820 (Fla. 1962).

Firearm Definitions
Florida vs. Federal

Firearms

Florida Stat. § 790.001(9)

"Firearm" means any weapon (including a starter gun) which will, is designed to, or may readily be converted to expel a projectile by the action of an explosive; the frame or receiver of any such weapon; any firearm muffler or firearm silencer; any destructive device; or any machine gun. The term "firearm" does not include an antique firearm unless the antique firearm is used in the commission of a crime.

Federal 18 *U.S.C.* § 921(a)(3)

The term ***"firearm"*** means: (A) any weapon (including a starter gun) which will or is designed to or may readily be converted to expel a projectile by the action of an explosive; (B) the frame or receiver of any such weapon; (C) any firearm muffler or firearm silencer; or (D) any destructive device.

Handguns

Florida Stat. § 790.001(10)

"Handgun" means a firearm capable of being carried and used by one hand, such as a pistol or revolver.

Federal 18 *U.S.C.* § 921(a)(30)

The term ***"handgun"*** means—(A) a firearm which has a short stock and is designed to be held and fired by the use of a single hand; and (B) any combination of parts from which a firearm described in subparagraph (A) can be assembled.

Shotguns; Rifles

Florida: Not formally defined in the Florida statutes.

Federal 18 *U.S.C.* § 921(a)(5) / 18 *U.S.C.* § 921(a)(7)

Shotgun: The term "shotgun" means a weapon designed or redesigned, made or remade, and intended to be fired from the shoulder and designed or redesigned and made or remade to use the energy of an explosive to fire through a smooth bore either a number of ball shot or a single projectile for each single pull of the trigger.

Rifle: The term "rifle" means a weapon designed or redesigned, made or remade, and intended to be fired from the shoulder and designed or redesigned and made or remade to use the energy of an explosive to fire only a single projectile through a rifled bore for each single pull of the trigger.

Curios; Black powder guns / Antique guns

The ATF has recognized only complete, assembled firearms as curios or relics. To be recognized as a curio or relic, firearms must fall within one of the following categories:

1. Firearms manufactured at least 50 years prior the current date, but not including replicas thereof;

2. Firearms certified by the curator of a municipal, state, or federal museum which exhibits firearms to be curios or relics of museum interest; and

3. Firearms which derive a substantial part of their monetary value from the fact that they are novel, rare, or bizarre or from the fact of their association with some historical figure, period, or event.[18]

Florida Stat. § 790.001(2)

"Antique firearm" means any firearm manufactured in or before 1918 (including any matchlock, flintlock, percussion cap, or similar early type of ignition system) or replica thereof, whether actually manufactured before or after the year 1918, and also any firearm using fixed ammunition manufactured in or before 1918, for which ammunition is no longer manufactured in the United States and is not readily available in the ordinary channels of commercial trade.

Federal 18 *U.S.C.* § 921(a)(16)

The term ***"Antique Firearms"*** means—(A) any firearm (including any firearm with a matchlock, flintlock, percussion cap, or similar type of ignition system) manufactured on or before 1898; or (B) any replica of any firearm described in subparagraph (A) if such replica—(i) is not designed or redesigned for using rimfire or conventional centerfire fixed ammunition, or (ii) uses rimfire or conventional centerfire fixed ammunition which is no longer manufactured in the United States and which is not readily available in the ordinary channels of commercial trade; or

[18] https://www.atf.gov/firearms/qa/what-firearms-are-considered-be-curio-and-relic-firearms

(C) any muzzle loading rifle, muzzle loading shotgun, or muzzle loading pistol, which is designed to use black powder, or a black powder substitute, and which cannot use fixed ammunition.

For purposes of this subparagraph, the term "antique firearm" shall not include any weapon which incorporates a firearm frame or receiver, any firearm which is converted into a muzzle loading weapon, or any muzzle loading weapon which can be readily converted to fire fixed ammunition by replacing the barrel, bolt, breechblock, or any combination thereof.

Machine guns

Florida Stat. § 790.001(13).

"Machine gun" means any firearm which shoots, or is designed to shoot, automatically more than one shot, without manually reloading, by a single function of the trigger.

Federal 26 *U.S.C.* § 5845(b)

The term ***"machine gun"*** means any weapon which shoots, is designed to shoot, or can be readily restored to shoot, automatically more than one shot, without manual reloading, by a single function of the trigger. The term shall also include the frame or receiver of any such weapon, any part designed and intended solely and exclusively, or combination of parts designed and intended, for use in converting a weapon into a machinegun, and any combination of parts from which a machinegun can be assembled if such parts are in the possession or under the control of a person.

NOTE: Bump Stocks. On June 14, 2024, the United States Supreme Court in *Garland, A.G., v. Cargill*, 602 *U.S.* 406, 144 *S.Ct.* 222 (2024) held that a semiautomatic rifle equipped with a bump stock does not meet the definition of a "machinegun" as defined under 26 *U.S.C.* § 5845(b) of the National Firearms Act because the Court determined it cannot fire more than one shot by a single function of the trigger and, even if it could, it does not do so automatically.

A "bump stock" is an accessory that attaches to a semi-automatic firearm to increase the firing rate, approaching the speed of some machine guns.

It is important to note that although non-mechanical bump stocks are no longer prohibited as a machine gun under federal law, certain state and local laws still prohibit the use, possession and/or transfer of non-mechanical bump stocks.

The ban on bump stocks was a result of the 2017 Las Vegas mass shooting, where the shooter used a bump stock to fire hundreds of rounds into the crowd. The ATF defined bump stocks as machine guns, which are tightly regulated under federal law. This ruling effectively legalized bump stocks in Texas, Louisiana, and Mississippi.

Short-barrel rifles and shotguns

Florida Stat. § 790.001(16), (17)

"Short-barreled rifle" means a rifle having one or more barrels less than 16 inches in length and any weapon made from a rifle (whether by alteration, modification, or otherwise) if such weapon as modified has an overall length of less than 26 inches.

"Short-barreled shotgun" means a shotgun having one or more barrels less than 18 inches in length and any weapon made from a shotgun (whether by alteration, modification, or otherwise) if such weapon as modified has an overall length of less than 26 inches.

Federal 18 *U.S.C.* § 921(a)(6) / 18 U.S. Code § 921(a)(8)

The term ***"short-barreled rifle"*** means a rifle having one or more barrels less than sixteen inches in length and any weapon made from a rifle (whether by alteration, modification, or otherwise) if such weapon, as modified, has an overall length of less than twenty-six inches.

The term ***"short-barreled shotgun"*** means a shotgun having one or more barrels less than eighteen inches in length and any weapon made from a shotgun (whether by alteration, modification or otherwise) if such a weapon as modified, has an overall length of less than twenty-six inches.

The martial artist's hands and feet.

In *Dixon v. State,*[19] the court held that, "in general, bare hands (like bare feet) are not deadly weapons for purposes of alleging or proving the crime of aggravated battery." The issue of whether the bare hands or feet of a person with special skills and training in martial arts to kill or inflict deadly force with them can be deemed "deadly weapons" "is reserved for future consideration. But, in this case, there was no allegation or proof Dixon had any such skills or training."[20]

Compare *R.V. v. State,*[21] where the court held that "a nunchaku ('num-chucks'), a potentially lethal device which originated from the martial arts, is a deadly weapon. Unlike other common objects that may be deadly only because of their use or threatened use, the sole modern use of a nunchaku is to cause great bodily harm. Appellants, who carried the nunchaku on their persons in a concealed manner, were properly adjudicated delinquent for carrying a concealed weapon."

In *United States v. Rocha,*[22] Rocha used only his bare hands in attacking Fischer. At trial, the government argued that Rocha used both his hands and the concrete floor as dangerous weapons in assaulting Fischer. The Court of Appeals disagreed, emphasizing that "most states have determined that body parts cannot be considered a dangerous or deadly weapon."[23]

---

[19] *Dixon v. State*, 603 So.2d 570 (1992).

[20] *Dixon v. State*, 603 So.2d 570, 572 (1992); *see also Davis v. State*, 565 So. 2d 826 (Fla. 5th DCA 1990), where the court determined that the indictment, which alleged the defendant kicked the victim with his foot, failed to charge him with aggravated battery because no "deadly weapon" was alleged to have been used. The court acknowledged, however, that had the information alleged the defendant wore a heavy shoe or boot which could have inflicted deadly force, the aggravated battery charge would have passed legal muster.

[21] *R.V. v. State*, 497 So.2d 912 (Fla. 3d DCA 1986).

[22] *United States v. Rocha*, 598 F.3d 1144 (9th Cir. 2010).

[23] *See State v. Flemming*, 19 S.W.3d 195 (Tenn. 2000) (fists and feet); *People v. Owusu*, 93 N.Y.2d 398, 712 N.E.2d 1228, 690 N.Y.S.2d 863 (N.Y. 1999) (teeth); *State v. Bachelor*, 6 Neb. Ct. App. 426, 575 N.W.2d 625 (Neb. Ct. App. 1998) (teeth); *Ex Parte Cobb*, 703 So. 2d 871 (Ala. 1996) (fists or other body parts); *People v. Aguilar*, 945 P.2d 1204 (Cal. 1997) (bare hands or feet); *State v. Townsend*, 865 P.2d 972 (Idaho 1993) (hands); *State v. Frey*, 505 N.W.2d 786 (WiS. Ct. App. 1993) (hands); *Dixon v. State*, 603 So. 2d 570 (Fla. Dist. Ct. App. 1992) (bare hands); *State v. Gordon*, 778 P.2d 1204 (Ariz. 1989) (fists); *Seiter v. State*, 719 S.W.2d 141 (Mo. Ct. App.

§ 7.2. Penalties

Relevant penalties are set forth in **§ 775.082 (imprisonment); and § 775.083 (fines):**

1° Felony—a term of imprisonment 30 years to life and a fine not to exceed $10,000.

2° Felony—a term of imprisonment not exceeding 15 years and a fine not to exceed $10,000.

3° Felony—a term of imprisonment not exceeding 5 years and a fine not to exceed $5,000.

1° Misdemeanor—a term of imprisonment not exceeding 1 year and a fine not to exceed $1,000.

2° Misdemeanor—a term of imprisonment not exceeding 60 days and a fine not to exceed $500.

---

§ 7.3. Carrying of concealed weapons/firearms

(a) With a license

§ 790.01. Carrying of concealed weapons or concealed firearms.

(1) A person is authorized to carry a concealed weapon or concealed firearm, as that term is defined in § 790.06(1), if he or she:

(a) Is licensed under § 790.06; or

(b) Is not licensed under § 790.06, but otherwise satisfies the criteria for receiving and maintaining such a license under § 790.06(2)(a)—(f) and (i)—(n), (3), and (10).

1986) (hands); *People v. Bias*, 475 N.E.2d 253, 86 Ill. Dec. 256 (Ill. App. Ct. 1985) (a sharp fingernail); *Roney v. Commonwealth*, 695 S.W.2d 863 (Ky. 1985) (fists and body parts); *Commonwealth v. Davis*, 406 N.E.2d 417 (MasS.Ct. App. 1980) (fists and teeth); *People v. Van Diver*, 263 N.W.2d 370 (Mich. Ct. App. 1977) (bare hands); *State v. Ireland*, 447 P.2d 375 (Utah 1968) (hands); *State v. Calvin*, 24 So. 2d 467 (La. 1945) (bare hands and teeth); *Bean v. State*, 138 P.2d 563 (Okla. Crim. App. 1943) (fists); *Warren v. State*, 114 S.W.705 (Ark. 1908) (fists).

(2) Except as provided in subsection (5), a person who does not meet the criteria in subsection (1) and who carries a concealed weapon or electric weapon or device, as those terms are defined in § 790.001, on or about his or her person commits a ***misdemeanor of the first degree***. . . .

(3) Except as provided in subsection (5), a person who does not meet the criteria in subsection (1) and who carries a concealed firearm, as that term is defined in § 790.001, on or about his or her person commits a ***felony of the third degree***. . . .

(4) In any prosecution for a violation of subsection (2) or subsection (3), the state bears the burden of proving, as an element of the offense, both that a person is not licensed under § 790.06 and that he or she is ineligible to receive and maintain such a license under the criteria listed in § 790.06(2)(a)-(f) and (i)-(n), (3), and (10).

(5) A person does not violate this section if he or she

(a) Is lawfully in possession of a concealed weapon or a concealed firearm * * * and carries such concealed weapon or concealed firearm, on or about his or her person while in the act of evacuating during a mandatory evacuation order issued during a state of emergency declared by the Governor * * *.

(b) Carries for purposes of lawful self-defense, in a concealed manner:

1. A self-defense chemical spray.

2. A nonlethal stun gun or dart-firing stun gun or other nonlethal electric weapon or device that is designed solely for defensive purposes.

(6) This section does not preclude any prosecution for the use of an electric weapon or device, a dart-firing stun gun, or a self-defense chemical spray during the commission of any criminal offense under § 790.07, § 790.10, § 790.23, or § 790.235, or for any other criminal offense.

Rev. § 5, ch. 2004-286; § 2, ch. 2006-298; § 1, ch. 2015-44; § 5, ch. 2023-18.

(b) Without a license

§ 790.013. Carrying of concealed weapons or concealed firearms without a license.

A person who carries a concealed weapon or concealed firearm without a license as authorized under § 790.01(1)(b):

(1) Must carry valid identification at all times when he or she is in actual possession of a concealed weapon or concealed firearm and must display such identification upon demand by a law enforcement officer. A violation of this subsection is a noncriminal violation punishable by a $25 fine, payable to the clerk of the court.

(2) Is subject to § 790.06(12) in the same manner as a person who is licensed to carry a concealed weapon or concealed firearm.

Added § 6, ch. 2023-18; § 63, ch. 2024-2.

(c) In a vehicle

§ 790.25(4). Possession in private conveyance.

(a) Notwithstanding § 790.01, a person 18 years of age or older who is in lawful possession of a handgun or other weapon may possess such a handgun or weapon within the interior of a private conveyance if the handgun or weapon is securely encased or otherwise not readily accessible for immediate use. A person who possesses a handgun or other weapon as authorized under this paragraph may not carry the handgun or weapon on his or her person.

(b) This subsection does not prohibit a person from carrying a:

1. Legal firearm other than a handgun anywhere in a private conveyance when such firearm is being carried for a lawful use; or

2. Concealed weapon or concealed firearm on his or her person while in a private conveyance if he or she is authorized to carry a concealed weapon or concealed firearm under § 790.01(1).

(c) This subsection shall be liberally construed in favor of the lawful use, ownership, and possession of firearms and other weapons, including lawful self-defense as provided in § 776.012.

Rev. § 1, ch. 2019-77; § 20, ch. 2022-183; § 14, ch. 2023-18; § 5, ch. 2023-167.

(d) On a boat or vessel

Unlike many other states, Florida has hundreds of miles of beaches and beautiful waters for boating. In this state, *it is lawful* for a person without a Concealed Weapon/Firearm License (CWFL) to have a concealed handgun, rifle, or shotgun in their boat or ship. The definition of conveyance, as set forth below, includes not only motor vehicles and aircraft, but also any ship or vessel per Florida Statute §810.011(3). The same conditions apply to vessels as to cars. When you carry a concealed handgun in a boat or other vessel, follow the same rules as if it were in your car. Ensure the concealed handgun is securely encased or otherwise not readily accessible for immediate use, unless you have a CWFL

In pertinent part, Fla. Stat. § 810.011(3) provides:

> **(3)** ***"Conveyance"*** means any motor vehicle, ship, vessel, railroad vehicle or car, trailer, aircraft, or sleeping car; and "to enter a conveyance" includes taking apart any portion of the conveyance.

Once you are beyond the ***3-mile limit*** on the east coast, or the western edge of the Gulf Stream, or the ***9-mile limit*** (three leagues) on the Gulf Coast, you have entered international waters, where the regulations are eased.[24]

CAUTION: No firearms are allowed in restricted or secured Florida seaports. In this regard, Fla. Stat. § 311.12(3)(b) provides:

---

[24] *See Fla. Const.* Art. 2, § 1 (State Boundaries).

"Any person in a restricted area who has in his or her possession a concealed weapon, or who operate or has possession or control of a vehicle in or upon which a concealed weapon is placed or stored, commits a misdemeanor of the first degree . . ." Note that each seaport is required by law to post appropriate signs and markers on the premises notifying individuals that firearms are prohibited.

International waters. In international waters, the laws of the vessel's "Flag of Origin" govern. As a result, Florida law will govern a vessel registered in Florida. The Coast Guard may board an individual's vessel at any time and perform random searches. If this happens, a person should immediately inform officers that they are in possession of a firearm. The standard Coast Guard procedure is to document the serial number of any firearm the person has on board.

Foreign Ports. If you intend to dock in a foreign port, you should contact that country's consulate in advance to find out what their laws are regarding the possession of firearms on your boat or vessel. Various countries have strict firearm laws.

For example, should you decide to take the short trip from Fort Lauderdale to Bimini, Bahamas, be sure to be ready to present your passport, *and if you have a firearm (shotguns and handguns only), you must declare it* with the Bahamian Customs authorities. You must provide the serial number, the name of the manufacturer, plus an exact count of ammunition. While you are allowed to have a firearm on your boat, you cannot remove it. Weapons must be "under lock and key" at all times. In cases of emergencies, which require your departure by air, you must notify the Bahamian Police or Customs. They will accompany you to retrieve the firearm and present you with a receipt. Upon your return to the island, the Bahamian Police or Customs will escort you to your vessel and return your firearm. Any infraction of this law will be dealt with severely.[25]

---

[25] *See https://www.bahamas.com/getting-here/boating/boat-regulations.*

(e) Other lawful uses

§ 790.25(2). Lawful uses.

Notwithstanding §§ 790.01, 790.053, and 790.06, the following persons may own, possess, and lawfully use firearms and other weapons, ammunition, and supplies for lawful purposes if they are not otherwise prohibited from owning or possessing a firearm under state or federal law:

* * *

(h) A person engaged in fishing, camping, or lawful hunting or going to or returning from a fishing, camping, or lawful hunting expedition;

(i) A person engaged in the business of manufacturing, repairing, or dealing in firearms, or the agent or representative of any such person while engaged in the lawful course of such business;

(j) A person discharging a weapon or firearm for testing or target practice under safe conditions and in a safe place not prohibited by law or going to or from such place;

(k) A person discharging a weapon or firearm in a safe and secure indoor range for testing and target practice;

(l) A person traveling in a public conveyance when the weapon or firearm is securely encased and not in the person's manual possession;

(m) A person while carrying a handgun unloaded and in a secure wrapper, concealed or otherwise, from the place of purchase to his or her home or place of business or to a place of repair or back to his or her home or place of business;

(n) A person possessing weapons or firearms at his or her home or place of business;

Rev. § 1, ch. 2019-77; § 20, ch. 2022-183; § 14, ch. 2023-18; § 5, ch. 2023-167.

§ 7.4. Nonresidents; reciprocity

§ 790.015. Nonresidents; reciprocity.

(1) A nonresident of Florida may carry a concealed weapon or concealed firearm, as that term is defined in § 790.06(1), while in this state if the nonresident is a resident of the United States who is 21 years of age or older and he or she:

(a) Satisfies the criteria for receiving and maintaining a license to carry a concealed weapon or concealed firearm under § 790.06(2)(a)-(f) and (i)-(n), (3), and (10); or

(b) Has in his or her immediate possession a valid license to carry a concealed weapon or concealed firearm issued to the nonresident in his or her state of residence.

(2) A nonresident is subject to the same laws and restrictions with respect to carrying a concealed weapon or concealed firearm as a resident of Florida.

(3) If the resident of another state who is the holder of a valid license to carry a concealed weapon or concealed firearm issued in another state establishes legal residence in this state by:

(a) Registering to vote;

(b) Making a statement of domicile pursuant to § 222.17; or

(c) Filing for homestead tax exemption on property in this state, the license shall be recognized as valid for 90 days following the date on which the holder of the license establishes legal state residence.

(4) The requirement in subsection (1) that a nonresident be 21 years of age or older to carry a concealed weapon or concealed firearm does not apply to a person who: (a) Is a servicemember, as defined in § 250.01; or (b) Is a veteran of the United States Armed Forces who was discharged under honorable conditions.

Rev. § 2, ch. 2012-108; § 29, ch. 2022-183; § 7, ch. 2023-18.

---

https://www.usconcealedcarry.com/resources/ccw_reciprocity_map/fl-gun-laws

Florida
Concealed Carry Reciprocity Map

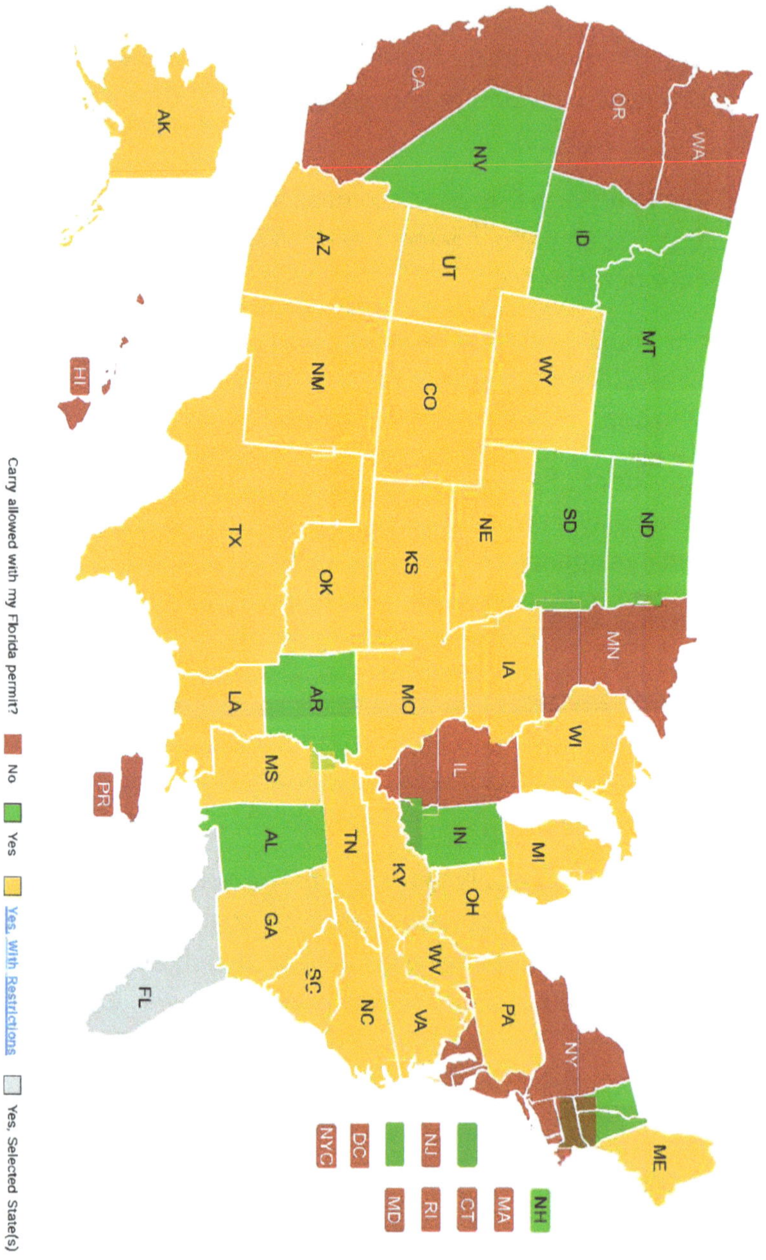

§ 7.5. Open carry

McDANIELS v. STATE

Court of Appeals of Florida, First District
419 So.3d 1180 (9/10/2025)

QUESTION: Does Florida's Open Carry Ban, §790.053, Florida Statutes, violate the Second Amendment's right to bear arms in public?

ANSWER: YES. "The Constitution protects the right to carry arms openly for self-defense. Florida's Open Carry Ban cannot be reconciled with that guarantee. Section 790.053, Florida Statutes, is therefore declared unconstitutional." *Id.* at 1194.

RATIONALE: "On the Fourth of July 2022, McDaniels stood at a major intersection in downtown Pensacola. He held a copy of the United States Constitution in one hand and waved at vehicles that drove by with his other hand. He also had a loaded handgun tucked inside his pants using an inside-the-waistband holster. The holstered firearm was visible to anyone who passed by, but McDaniels was not threatening anyone." *Id.* at 1183.

"When law enforcement officers arrived at the scene several hours later, McDaniels was cooperative. He explained that he wanted to take this case to the Supreme Court. When asked for identification, he gave them a copy of his Florida Concealed Carry permit. They advised him that while concealed carry was lawful, open carry was not." *Id.* The officers later obtained a warrant for McDaniels's arrest for openly carrying a firearm in violation of Florida's Open Carry Ban.

In this appeal, the court explained:

> Florida law generally makes it a crime for an ordinary, law-abiding, adult citizen to carry a firearm openly in public. Stanley Victor McDaniels was convicted under that law, and he now appeals. He contends that this open carry ban is incompatible with the Second Amendment's guarantee of the right to bear arms. Guided by the Constitution's text and this Nation's historical tradition of firearm regulation, *we agree.* We therefore declare the law unconstitutional, vacate McDaniels's conviction, and reverse his sentence.

Id. at 1182-83.

Following the United States Supreme Court's holding in *New York State Rifle & Pistol Association v. Bruen*, 597 *U.S.* 1, 142 S.*Ct.* 2111 (2021), the Florida Court of Appeals determined that the historical record "shows that our Nation did not regard concealed carry and open carry as interchangeable. The right to keep and bear arms did not extend to the carrying of weapons in secret, which was regarded as the practice of the cowardly and the disreputable and as incompatible with the legitimate exercise of the right of self-defense. Open carry, by contrast, was understood to be the manner of bearing arms that gave full effect to the rights secured by the Second Amendment." *Id.* at 1193.

"Because the Second Amendment's plain text encompasses the open carrying of firearms in public, that conduct is presumptively protected by the Constitution. . . . The historical record makes clear that open carry was regarded as the lawful and preferred mode of bearing arms, while concealed carry was viewed as dangerous to public safety and ineffective for self-defense." *Id.* at 1193-94.

"No historical tradition supports Florida's Open Carry Ban. To the contrary, history confirms that the right to bear arms in public necessarily includes the right to do so openly. That is not to say that open carry is absolute or immune from reasonable regulation. But what the State may not do is extinguish the right altogether for ordinary, law-abiding, adult citizens." *Id.* at 1194.

Accordingly, the court held that § 790.053, Florida Statutes is unconstitutional. It therefore reversed McDaniels's conviction and vacated his sentence.

§ 790.053. Open carrying of weapons.

Declared Unconstitutional

(1) Except as otherwise provided by law and in subsection (2), it is unlawful for any person to openly carry on or about his or her person any firearm or electric weapon or device. It is not a violation of this section for a person who carries a concealed firearm as authorized in § 790.01(1) to briefly and openly display the firearm to the ordinary sight of another person, unless the firearm is intentionally displayed in an angry or threatening manner, not in necessary self-defense.

In A Nutshell **OPEN & CONSTITUTIONAL CARRY:**

(1) The legality of firearms possession in Florida had a critical change as of September 25, 2025. After the Florida Court of Appeals (First District) struck down the state's historical "Open Carry" ban in ***McDaniels v. State*** on September 10, 2025, ***declaring § 790.053, Fla. Stat., unconstitutional,*** Florida's attorney general issued a directive, advising prosecutors and law enforcement officers not to enforce the ban.

September 25, 2025, marked the deadline for the state's appellate judges to challenge the decision allowing open carry earlier in the month, which they declined to do. Said the Attorney General: ***"Effectively, the McDaniels decision is now the law of the State."***

(2) In short, adults who can lawfully possess a firearm may now carry it openly in most public places, subject to important limits. This new ruling applies the U.S. Supreme Court's framework from *New York State Rifle & Pistol Association v. Bruen* (2022). Caution: Nothing in the *McDaniels* decision authorizes menacing displays—defined under Fla. Stat. § 790.10 as exhibiting a firearm in a rude, careless, angry, or threatening manner—or possession by prohibited persons, such as convicted felons, those under domestic violence injunctions, or individuals adjudicated mentally ill.

(3) Recall that since July 1, 2023, qualifying individuals have been able to carry concealed weapons without a license (also called "constitutional carry"), pursuant to HB 543, Ch. 2023-18 (§ 790.013, Florida Statutes). That law did not legalize carry everywhere; *a long list of restricted locations still applies for both Concealed and Open Carry,* including, for example, in areas of restaurants primarily devoted to alcohol service. For the list of restricted locations, refer to Section 7.7 (this text) and §790.06(12)(a).

(4) Note that private property owners can still prohibit firearms on their premises, and refusals to leave can lead to trespass charges, including armed trespass (a third-degree felony). Thus, Florida's new Open Carry reality does not override a private employer's right to prohibit firearms on their own private property. Any person carrying a firearm who violates a private property owner's warning to depart will be committing armed trespass, a third-degree felony, *See* § 810.08(2)(c), Fla. Stat.

OPEN CARRY

Based on the guidance issued by FL Attorney General James Uthmeier, expected to take effect on September 25, 2025, some key points relating to the open carry of guns in the state of Florida are as follows:

Some areas where open (or concealed) carry is **PROHIBITED** include:

- Board of County Commission Meetings
- City Commission/Council Meetings
- Courthouses
- Police Stations and Sheriff's Offices
- Bars (or bar areas of restaurants)
- Schools, School-Sponsored Events, or Property of any school, school bus or school bus stop
- Colleges or other higher education institutions

At the **discretion of the owners***, you MAY or MAY NOT open carry in **privately owned** establishments such as:

- Grocery Stores
- Retail Stores
- Restaurants (dining areas only, not bar areas)

Please note:** If a person refuses to leave after having been asked to do so by the business, the person commits the crime of **armed trespass, *which is a felony.

§ 7.6. Carrying of concealed weapons/ firearms/licensing

§ 790.06. License to carry concealed weapon or concealed firearm.

(1) (a) For the purposes of this section, the term "concealed weapon or concealed firearm" means a handgun, electric weapon or device, tear gas gun, knife, or billie, but does not include a machine gun as that term is defined in § 790.001.

(b) The Department of Agriculture and Consumer Services is authorized to issue licenses to carry concealed weapons or concealed firearms to persons qualified as provided in this section. Each license must bear a color photograph of the licensee.

(c) Licenses are valid throughout the state for 7 years after the date of issuance. A licensee must carry valid identification at all times in which the licensee is in actual possession of a concealed weapon or concealed firearm and must display such identification upon demand by a law enforcement officer. Violations of the provisions of this subsection shall constitute a noncriminal violation with a penalty of $25, payable to the clerk of the court.

(a) Qualifications

§ 790.06 further provides:

* * * *

(2) The Department of Agriculture and Consumer Services shall issue a license if the applicant:

(a) Is a resident of the United States and a citizen of the United States or a permanent resident alien of the United States, as determined by the United States Bureau of Citizenship and Immigration Services, or is a consular security official of a foreign government that maintains diplomatic relations and treaties of commerce, friendship, and navigation with the United States and is certified as such by the foreign government and by the appropriate embassy in this country;

(b) Is 21 years of age or older;

(c) Does not suffer from a physical infirmity which prevents the safe handling of a weapon or firearm;

(d) Is not ineligible to possess a firearm pursuant to § 790.23 by virtue of having been convicted of a felony;

(e) Has not been: [Found guilty of a crime relating to controlled substances within a 3-year period immediately preceding the date on which the application is submitted; or committed for the abuse of a controlled substance.];

(f) Does not chronically and habitually use alcoholic beverages or other substances to the extent that his or her normal faculties are impaired[;]

(g) Desires a legal means to carry a concealed weapon or concealed firearm for lawful self-defense[.]

(b) Training requirements

§ 790.06 further provides:

* * * *

(h) Demonstrates competence with a firearm by any one of the following:

1. Completion of any hunter education or hunter safety course approved by the Fish and Wildlife Conservation Commission or a similar agency of another state;

2. Completion of any National Rifle Association firearms safety or training course;

3. Completion of any firearms safety or training course or class available to the general public offered by a law enforcement agency, junior college, college, or private or public institution or organization or firearms training school, using instructors certified by the National Rifle Association, Criminal Justice Standards and Training Commission, or the Department of Agriculture and Consumer Services;

4. Completion of any law enforcement firearms safety or training course or class offered for security guards, investigators, special deputies, or any division or subdivision of a law enforcement agency or security enforcement;

5. Presents evidence of equivalent experience with a firearm through participation in organized shooting competition or military service;

6. Is licensed or has been licensed to carry a concealed weapon or concealed firearm in this state or a county or municipality of this state, unless such license has been revoked for cause; or

7. Completion of any firearms training or safety course or class conducted by a state-certified or National Rifle Association certified firearms instructor;

A photocopy of a certificate of completion of any of the courses or classes; an affidavit from the instructor, school, club, organization, or group that conducted or taught such course or class attesting to the completion of the course or class by the applicant; or a copy of any document that shows completion of the course or class or evidences participation in firearms competition shall constitute evidence of qualification under this paragraph. * * *

(c) Disqualifications

§ 790.06 further provides:

* * * *

(i) Has not been adjudicated an incapacitated person under § 744.331, or similar laws of any other state. An applicant who has been granted relief from firearms disabilities pursuant to § 790.065(2)(a)4.d. or pursuant to the law of the state in which the adjudication occurred is deemed not to have been adjudicated an incapacitated person under this paragraph;

(j) Has not been committed to a mental institution * * *. An applicant who has been granted relief from firearms disabilities pursuant to § 790.065(2)(a)4.d. or pursuant to the law of the state in which the commitment occurred is deemed not to have been committed in a mental institution under this paragraph;

(k) Has not had adjudication of guilt withheld or imposition of sentence suspended on any felony unless 3 years have elapsed since probation or any other conditions set by the court have been fulfilled, or expunction has occurred;

(l) Has not had adjudication of guilt withheld or imposition of sentence suspended on any misdemeanor crime of domestic violence unless 3 years have elapsed since probation or any other conditions set by the court have been fulfilled, or the record has been expunged;

(m) Has not been issued an injunction that is currently in force and effect and that restrains the applicant from committing acts of domestic violence or acts of repeat violence; and

(n) Is not prohibited from purchasing or possessing a firearm by any other provision of Florida or federal law.

(d) Weapon/firearm applications

§ 790.06 further provides:

* * * *

(4) The application shall be completed, under oath, on a form adopted by the Department of Agriculture and Consumer Services and shall include:

(a) The name, address, place of birth, date of birth, and race of the applicant;

(b) A statement that the applicant is in compliance with criteria contained within subsections (2) and (3);

(c) A statement that the applicant has been furnished a copy of or a website link to this chapter and is knowledgeable of its provisions;

(d) A conspicuous warning that the application is executed under oath and that a false answer to any question, or the submission of any false document by the applicant, subjects the applicant to criminal prosecution[;]

(e) A statement that the applicant desires a concealed weapon or concealed firearms license as a means of lawful self-defense; and

(f) Directions for an applicant who is a servicemember * * * to request expedited processing of his or her application.

(5) The applicant shall submit to the Department of Agriculture and Consumer Services or an approved tax collector pursuant to § 790.0625 [various items, including a completed application, a nonrefundable license fee, a full set of fingerprints, a photocopy of a certificate of training/education, a recent color photograph of the applicant.]

* * * *

(c) The Department of Agriculture and Consumer Services shall, within 90 days after the date of receipt of the items listed in subsection (5): **1.** Issue the license; or **2.** Deny the application based solely on the ground that the applicant fails to qualify under the criteria listed in subsection (2) or subsection (3). * * *

* * * *

(8) Within 30 days after the changing of a permanent address, or within 30 days after having a license lost or destroyed, the licensee shall notify the Department of Agriculture and Consumer Services of such change. Failure to notify the Department of Agriculture and Consumer Services pursuant to the provisions of this subsection shall constitute a noncriminal violation with a penalty of $25.

(9) In the event that a concealed weapon or concealed firearm license is lost or destroyed, the license shall be automatically invalid, and the person to whom the same was issued may, upon payment of $15 to the Department of Agriculture and Consumer Services, obtain a duplicate, or substitute thereof, upon furnishing a notarized statement to the Department of Agriculture and Consumer Services that such license has been lost or destroyed.

* * * *

(11)(a) At least 90 days before the expiration date of the license, the Department of Agriculture and Consumer Services shall mail to each licensee a written notice of the expiration and a renewal form prescribed by the Department of Agriculture and Consumer Services. * * *

---

§ 7.7. Prohibited/restricted areas for open/concealed carry

§ 790.06 further provides:

* * * *

(12)(a) A license issued under this section does not authorize any person to openly carry a handgun or carry a concealed weapon or concealed firearm into:

1. Any place of nuisance as defined in § 823.05;

2. Any police, sheriff, or highway patrol station;

3. Any detention facility, prison, or jail;

4. Any courthouse;

5. Any courtroom, except that nothing in this section precludes a judge from carrying a concealed weapon or concealed firearm or determining who will carry a concealed weapon or concealed firearm in his or her courtroom;

6. Any polling place;

7. Any meeting of the governing body of a county, public school district, municipality, or special district;

8. Any meeting of the Legislature or a committee thereof;

9. Any school, college, or professional athletic event not related to firearms;

10. Any elementary or secondary school facility or administration building;

11. Any career center;

12. Any portion of an establishment licensed to dispense alcoholic beverages for consumption on the premises, which portion of the establishment is primarily devoted to such purpose;

13. Any college or university facility unless the licensee is a registered student, employee, or faculty member of such college or university and the weapon is a stun gun or nonlethal electric weapon or device designed solely for defensive purposes and the weapon does not fire a dart or projectile;

14. The inside of the passenger terminal and sterile area of any airport, provided that no person shall be prohibited from carrying any legal firearm into the terminal, which firearm is encased for shipment for purposes of checking such firearm as baggage to be lawfully transported on any aircraft; or

15. Any place where the carrying of firearms is prohibited by federal law.

(b) A person licensed under this section is not prohibited from carrying or storing a firearm in a vehicle for lawful purposes.

(c) This section does not modify the terms or conditions of §790.251(7).

(d) Any person who knowingly and willfully violates any provision of this subsection commits a misdemeanor of the second degree, punishable as provided in § 775.082 or § 775.083.

* * * *

Rev. § 39, ch. 2017-85; § 1, ch. 2021-200; § 30, ch. 2022-183; § 10, ch. 2023-18.

---

§ 7.8. Other areas of interest

(a) Carrying a firearm into a casino or on Indian lands

Generally, Florida law, both criminal and civil, controls whether a person can carry a firearm onto the lands owned by America's indigenous population. In this regard, FLA. STAT. § 285.16 provides:

285.16 Civil and criminal jurisdiction; Indian reservation.

(1) The State of Florida hereby assumes jurisdiction over criminal offenses committed by or against Indians or other persons within Indian reservations and over civil causes of actions between Indians or other persons or to which Indians or other persons are parties rising within Indian reservations.

(2) The civil and criminal laws of Florida shall obtain on all Indian reservations in this state and shall be enforced in the same manner as elsewhere throughout the state.

Therefore, since the concealed carry of a firearm on Native American land within the State of Florida is not specifically prohibited anywhere in federal or state law, a CWFL holder is allowed to carry a firearm on all Native American lands within the state.

Naturally, property rights still apply. A property owner can restrict the possession and carrying of a firearm on their property, so even if you have a CWFL, if you are asked to leave because you are carrying a firearm and you refuse, you can be arrested for trespassing.

Regarding other laws related to firearms and other weapons on Native American Land, 18 *U.S.C.* § 1165 prohibits hunting, trapping, or fishing on tribal property without lawful authority or permission from the tribe and imposes the penalties of forfeiture of any and all game, peltries, or fish, in addition to imprisonment up to 90 days.[26] In addition, 15 *U.S.C.* § 1243 makes it illegal to manufacture, sell, or possess a switchblade knife, and imposes a fine of not more than $2,000 or imprisonment for not more than five years, or both.

(b) Carrying a firearm into a religious institution

Generally, Florida law allows people to carry their concealed weapons into churches, synagogues, mosques, and other religious institutions. The revised law provides that if you own a gun, you can now take it with you to church. However, the law does not limit the private property rights of churches, synagogues, or other religious institutions to exercise control over their property regarding firearms.

---

[26] *See also Quechan Tribe of Indians v. Rowe*, 531 F.2d 408 (9th Cir. 1976) (Officer Buker of the Bureau of Indian Affairs had the authority and responsibility to enforce federal and tribal laws pursuant to 18 *U.S.C.* § 1165. That authority extended to non-Indians and clothed him with the legal power to prevent non-Indians from hunting on the reservation without consent of the tribe. *See also id.* at 410 (The Quechan Tribe "has the right to control, regulate and license hunting and fishing on the reservation.").

In this regard, § 790.06(13) provides:

(13) Notwithstanding any other law, for the purposes of safety, security, personal protection, or any other lawful purpose, a person licensed under this section may carry a concealed weapon or concealed firearm on property owned, rented, leased, borrowed, or lawfully used by a church, synagogue, or other religious institution. This subsection does not limit the private property rights of a church, synagogue, or other religious institution to exercise control over property that the church, synagogue, or other religious institution owns, rents, leases, borrows, or lawfully uses.

(c) Carrying a firearm onto a private aircraft

Generally, you are allowed to bring firearms and weapons on board a private jet charter. In this regard, the Transportation Security Administration (TSA) says that travelers may only transport unloaded firearms. These firearms should be stored in a locked hard-sided case that must be checked and stored in the luggage hold of the aircraft. In other words, you cannot have your firearm accessible to you in the cabin. Also, you may not carry any related firearm components with you into the cabin, including receivers, clips, magazines, ammunition, or firearm frames.

However, private jet charters add a little bit of flexibility for their passengers. You can receive permission from the charter operator to bring your firearm on board the aircraft and be exempt from the above TSA regulations, although you will still be subject to regulations set forth by the charter operator or airport. You will need to inform your charter operator of your desire to travel with your firearm. Advanced notice can mitigate potential delays in your flight service.

Also, keep in mind that your firearms will be subject to the laws of the state or country to which you are flying. If you're traveling to another country, customs officers will likely want to check your gun license. Having a copy within arm's reach can reduce waiting time for your departure or arrival.

(d) Firearms and parking lots

Fla. Stat. 790.251, fondly known as the "Parking Lot" law, makes it unlawful for a business or an employer to prohibit the use of parking areas to customers or employees who keep a lawful firearm and ammunition in their locked vehicle. In pertinent part, the statute provides:

*   *   *   *

(2) Definitions. As used in this section, the term:

(a) "Parking lot" means any property that is used for parking motor vehicles and is available to customers, employees, or invitees for temporary or long-term parking or storage of motor vehicles.

*   *   *   *

(4) Prohibited acts. No public or private employer may violate the constitutional rights of any customer, employee, or invitee as provided in paragraphs (a)-(e):

(a) No public or private employer may prohibit any customer, employee, or invitee from possessing any legally owned firearm when such firearm is lawfully possessed and locked inside or locked to a private motor vehicle in a parking lot and when the customer, employee, or invitee is lawfully in such area.

(b) No public or private employer may violate the privacy rights of a customer, employee, or invitee by verbal or written inquiry regarding the presence of a firearm inside or locked to a private motor vehicle in a parking lot or by an actual search of a private motor vehicle in a parking lot to ascertain the presence of a firearm within the vehicle. * * * A search of a private motor vehicle in the parking lot of a public or private employer to ascertain the presence of a firearm within the vehicle may only be conducted by on-duty law enforcement personnel, based upon due process and must comply with constitutional protections.

(c) No public or private employer shall condition employment upon . . .

> **2.** Any agreement by an employee or a prospective employee that prohibits an employee from keeping a legal firearm locked inside or locked to a private motor vehicle in a parking lot when such firearm is kept for lawful purposes.

(d) No public or private employer shall prohibit or attempt to prevent any customer, employee, or invitee from entering the parking lot of the employer's place of business because the customer's, employee's, or invitee's private motor vehicle contains a legal firearm being carried for lawful purposes, that is out of sight within the customer's, employee's, or invitee's private motor vehicle.

(e) No public or private employer may terminate the employment of or otherwise discriminate against an employee, or expel a customer or invitee for exercising his or her constitutional right to keep and bear arms or for exercising the right of self-defense as long as a firearm is never exhibited on company property for any reason other than lawful defensive purposes.

* * * *

---

§ 7.9. Interstate transportation of firearms

Federal law regulates interstate transportation of firearms. As such, you are authorized to lawfully transport your firearms from state to state, even if some of the pass-through states would otherwise prohibit it. In this regard, federal law provides:

18 U.S.C. § 926A. Interstate transportation of firearms

Notwithstanding any other provision of any law or any rule or regulation of a State or any political subdivision thereof, any person who is not otherwise prohibited by this chapter [18 U.S.C. §§ 921 ***et seq***.] from transporting, shipping, or receiving a firearm ***shall be entitled to transport a firearm for any lawful purpose*** from any place where he may lawfully possess and carry such firearm to any other place where he may lawfully possess and carry such firearm if, during such transportation the firearm is unloaded, and neither the firearm nor any ammunition being transported is readily accessible or is directly accessible from the passenger compartment of such transporting vehicle: ***Provided,*** That in the case of a vehicle without a compartment separate from the driver's compartment the firearm or ammunition shall be contained in a locked container other than the glove compartment or console.[27]

In A Nutshell

YOU CAN TRANSPORT A FIREARM ACROSS STATE LINES:

(1) If you are legally allowed to possess it in both the state of origin and destination;

(2) The firearm must be unloaded during transportation;

(3) The firearm and ammunition must not be readily accessible or directly accessible from the passenger compartment of the vehicle; and

(4) If the vehicle doesn't have a compartment separate from the driver's compartment, the firearm and ammunition must be in a locked container other than the glove compartment or console.

CAUTION: Be sure to check state and local laws to ensure that moving the firearms into the new state is legal.

---

[27] Note that there cannot be overnight stays. In this respect, in *Revell v. Port Auth.*, 598 *F.*3d 128 (3d Cir. 2010), the court held that the firearm owner's arrest under New Jersey's gun laws did not violate the law, as 18 *U.S.C.* § 926A did not immunize owner's transportation of firearm and ammunition through New Jersey because the owner missed his flight and had possession of luggage containing his firearm and ammunition during overnight stay.

§ 7.10. Mandatory waiting period[28]

§ 790.0655. Purchase and delivery of firearms; mandatory waiting period; exceptions; penalties.

(1)(a) A mandatory waiting period is imposed between the purchase and delivery of a firearm. The mandatory waiting period is 3 days,[29] excluding weekends and legal holidays, or expires upon the completion of the records checks required under § 790.065, whichever occurs later. . . .

(b) Records of firearm sales must be available for inspection by any law enforcement agency . . . during normal business hours.

(2) ***The waiting period does not apply in the following circumstances:***

(a) ***When a firearm is being purchased by a holder of a concealed weapons or concealed firearms license issued under § 790.06.***

(b) ***To a trade-in of another firearm.***

(c) To the purchase of a rifle or shotgun, upon a person's successfully completing a minimum of a 16-hour hunter safety course and possessing a hunter safety certification card issued under § 379.3581. . . .

(d) When a rifle or shotgun is being purchased by a law enforcement officer or correctional officer * * * or a servicemember[.]

(3) It is a felony of the third degree . . . : **(a)** For any retailer, or any employee or agent of a retailer, to deliver a firearm before the expiration of the waiting period, subject to the exceptions provided in subsection (2)[, or] **(b)** For a purchaser to obtain delivery of a firearm by fraud, false pretense, or false representation.

Rev. § 12, ch. 2018-3; § 33, ch. 2022-183; § 11, ch. 2023-18.

---

[28] The Florida Constitution, Art. I, § 8(b) also provides: "There shall be a mandatory period of three days, excluding weekends and legal holidays, between the purchase and delivery at retail of any handgun. For the purposes of this section, "purchase" means the transfer of money or other valuable consideration to the retailer, and "handgun" means a firearm capable of being carried and used by one hand, such as a pistol or revolver. Holders of a concealed weapon permit as prescribed in Florida law shall not be subject to the provisions of this paragraph."

[29] Private sales between individuals are not subject to the 3-day waiting period.

§ 7.11. Restrictions for minors

Florida's gun laws are more restrictive than what federal law requires. Its aim is to prevent minors from accessing weapons due to their potential lack of judgment and maturity.

§ 790.17. Furnishing weapons to minors under 18 years of age or furnishing firearms to minors under 18 years of age prohibited.

(1) A person who sells, hires, barters, lends, transfers, or gives any minor under 18 years of age any dirk, electric weapon or device, or other weapon, other than an ordinary pocketknife, without permission of the minor's parent or guardian, or sells, hires, barters, lends, transfers, or gives to any person of unsound mind an electric weapon or device or any dangerous weapon, other than an ordinary pocketknife, commits a ***misdemeanor of the first degree***[.]

(2)(a) A person may not knowingly or willfully sell or transfer a firearm to a minor under 18 years of age, except that a person may transfer ownership of a firearm to a minor with permission of the parent or guardian. A person who violates this paragraph commits a ***felony of the third degree***[.]

(b) The parent or guardian must maintain possession of the firearm except pursuant to § 790.22.

Rev. § 175, ch. 91-224; § 2, ch. 93-416.

790.22 Use of BB guns, air or gas-operated guns, or electric weapons or devices by minor under 16; limitation; possession of firearms by minor under 18 prohibited; penalties.

(1) The use for any purpose whatsoever of BB guns, air or gas-operated guns, or electric weapons or devices, by any minor ***under the age of 16 years*** is prohibited unless such use is under the supervision and in the presence of an adult who is acting with the consent of the minor's parent or guardian.

(2) Any adult responsible for the welfare of any child ***under the age of 16 years*** who knowingly permits such child to use or have in his or her possession any BB gun, air or gas-operated gun, electric weapon or device, or firearm in violation of the provisions of subsection (1) of this section commits a ***misdemeanor of the second degree***[.]

(3) A minor ***under 18 years of age*** may not possess a firearm, other than an unloaded firearm at his or her home, unless:

(a) The minor is engaged in a lawful hunting activity and is:

1. At least ***16 years of age***; or
2. Under ***16 years of age*** and supervised by an adult.

(b) The minor is engaged in a lawful marksmanship competition or practice or other lawful recreational shooting activity and is:

1. At least ***16 years of age***; or
2. Under ***16 years of age*** and supervised by an adult who is acting with the consent of the minor's parent or guardian.

(c) The firearm is unloaded and is being transported by the minor directly to or from an event authorized in paragraph (a) or paragraph (b).

(4)(a) Any parent or guardian of a minor, or other adult responsible for the welfare of a minor, who knowingly and willfully permits the minor to possess a firearm in violation of subsection (3) commits a ***felony of the third degree***[.]

*   *   *   *

(5)(a) A minor who violates subsection (3):

1. For a ***first offense,*** commits a ***misdemeanor of the first degree***; shall serve a period of detention of up to 5 days in a secure detention facility . . . ; and shall be required to perform 100 hours of community service or paid work as determined by the department.

2. For a ***second or subsequent offense***, commits a ***felony of the third degree***. For a second offense, the minor shall serve a period of detention of up to 21 days in a secure detention facility . . . , and shall be required to perform not less than 100 nor more than 250 hours of community service or paid work as determined by the department. ***For a third or subsequent offense,*** the minor shall be adjudicated delinquent and committed to a residential program. . . .

(b) In addition to the penalties for a violation of subsection (3): [the minor's driving privileges may be withheld, revoked or suspended.]

*   *   *   *

(6) Any firearm that is possessed or used by a minor in violation of this section shall be promptly seized by a law enforcement officer and disposed of in accordance with § 790.08(1)-(6).

(7) The provisions of this section are supplemental to all other provisions of law relating to the possession, use, or exhibition of a firearm.

Rev. § 33, ch. 2019-167; § 2, ch. 2023-87; § 2, ch. 2024-130; § 4, ch. 2024-133.

In A Nutshell

POSSESSION: Minors under 18 cannot possess a firearm, unless they are:

- At least 16 years old and participating in a lawful shooting activity;
- Under 16 years old and supervised by an adult with the minor's parent or guardian's consent;
- Transporting an unloaded firearm to or from a lawful shooting activity; or
- Possessing an unloaded firearm in their home

Purchase: No one under 21 years of age can purchase a firearm.

Sale: It is illegal to sell, deliver, or transfer a firearm to a minor under 18 years of age.

- **Furnishing:** Furnishing weapons to minors is a second-degree felony, punishable by up to 15 years in prison and a $10,000 fine.
- **Storage:** Adults are held culpable if they store or leave a loaded firearm within reach of a minor and the minor uses it to injure or kill themselves or others.

---

§ 7.12. Arrest for violations

§ 790.02. Officer to arrest without warrant and upon probable cause.

The carrying of a concealed weapon is declared a breach of peace, and any officer authorized to make arrests under the laws of this state may make arrests without warrant of persons violating the provisions of §790.01 when said officer has reasonable grounds or probable cause to believe that the offense of carrying a concealed weapon is being committed.

History.—§ 1, ch. 4929, 1901; GS 3263; RGS 5096; CGL 7198; § 3, ch. 69-306.

---

§ 7.13. Police exemption

§ 790.051. Officer exemption from licensing requirements.

Law enforcement officers are exempt from the licensing and penal provisions of this chapter when acting at any time within the scope or course of their official duties or when acting at any time in the line of or performance of duty.

History.—§ 11, ch. 69-306.

Notes

Chapter Eight
The Right To Keep And Bear Arms

§ 8.1. Second Amendment issues: U.S. Supreme Court

The right to keep and bear arms is among the "fundamental rights necessary to our system of ordered liberty."[30] As held in *New York State Rifle & Pistol Assn., Inc. v. Bruen*,[31] this right secures for Americans a means of self-defense.

"In the aftermath of the Civil War, Congress's desire to enable the newly freed slaves to defend themselves against former Confederates helped inspire the passage of the Fourteenth Amendment, which secured

[30] *McDonald v. Chicago*, 561 U. S. 742, 778, 130 S.Ct. 3020 (2010).
[31] *New York State Rifle & Pistol Assn., Inc. v. Bruen*, 597 U. S. 1, 17, 142 S.Ct. 2111 (2022).

the right to bear arms against interference by the States."[32] As a leading and early proponent of emancipation observed, "Disarm a community and you rob them of the means of defending life. Take away their weapons of defense and you take away the inalienable right of defending liberty."[33]

"Like most rights," though, "the right secured by the Second Amendment is not unlimited."[34] In *District of Columbia v. Heller,*[35] the Court held that the right applied to ordinary citizens within the home. However, this right is not one "to keep and carry any weapon whatsoever in any manner whatsoever and for whatever purpose." At the founding of this Nation, "the bearing of arms was subject to regulations ranging from rules about firearm storage to restrictions on gun use by drunken New Year's Eve revelers."[36]

In *New York State Rifle & Pistol Assn., Inc. v. Bruen,*[37] the Court addressed a New York law that provided that public-carry licenses may be issued only when an applicant demonstrated *a special need for self-defense.* The Court held that this State's licensing regime violated the Constitution because the Second and Fourteenth Amendments protected an individual's right to carry a handgun for self-defense outside the home. A State could not prevent law-abiding citizens from publicly carrying handguns because they had not demonstrated a "special need for self-defense."

At the time of the *Bruen* decision, the Court noted that 43 states are *"shall issue"* jurisdictions, where authorities must issue concealed-carry licenses whenever applicants satisfy certain threshold requirements, without granting licensing officials discretion to deny licenses based on a perceived lack of need or suitability. But in six States, including New

---

[32] *United States v. Rahimi*, 602 U.S. 680, 144 S.Ct. 1889, 1897 (2024) (citing *McDonald v. Chicago*, 561 U. S. 742, 771-76, 130 S.Ct. 3020 (2010) (holding that the right to keep and bear arms applies to the states through the Fourteenth Amendment)).

[33] Cong. Globe, 40th Cong., 2d Sess., 1967 (1868) (statement of Rep. Stevens).

[34] *District of Columbia v. Heller*, 554 U. S. 570, 626, 128 S.Ct. 2783 (2008).

[35] *District of Columbia v. Heller*, 554 U. S. 570, 128 S.Ct. 2783 (2008).

[36] *United States v. Rahimi*, 602 U.S. 680, 144 S.Ct. 1889, 1897 (2024) (Act of Mar. 1, 1783, 1783 Mass. Acts and Laws ch.13, pp. 218-219; 5 Colonial Laws of New York ch. 1501, pp. 244-246 (1894)).

[37] *New York State Rifle & Pistol Assn., Inc. v. Bruen*, 597 U. S. 1, 17, 142 S.Ct. 2111 (2022).

York, the government further conditions issuance of a license to carry on a citizen's showing of some additional *special or urgent need.* Because New York State issues public-carry licenses only when an applicant demonstrates a special need for self-defense, the Court held that the licensing regime violates the Constitution.

Beyond New York, carry permit laws in California, the District of Columbia, Hawaii, Maryland, Massachusetts and New Jersey all share New York's constitutional flaw of requiring the applicant to "demonstrate a special need for self-protection distinguishable from that of the general community." In this regard, the *Bruen* Court noted that the "special need" standard is "demanding." For example, living or working in an area "noted for criminal activity" does not suffice. "Rather, New York courts generally require evidence "of particular threats, attacks or other extraordinary danger to personal safety." This requirement, held the Court, violates the Second Amendment and Fourteenth Amendments.

Said the Court:

> The constitutional right to bear arms in public for self-defense is not "a second-class right, subject to an entirely different body of rules than the other Bill of Rights guarantees." . . . We know of no other constitutional right that an individual may exercise only after demonstrating to government officers some special need. That is not how the First Amendment works when it comes to unpopular speech or the free exercise of religion. It is not how the Sixth Amendment works when it comes to a defendant's right to confront the witnesses against him. And it is not how the Second Amendment works when it comes to public carry for self-defense.
>
> New York's proper-cause requirement violates the Fourteenth Amendment in that it prevents law-abiding citizens with ordinary self-defense needs from exercising their right to keep and bear arms.[38]

---

[38] *New York State Rifle & Pistol Assn., Inc. v. Bruen,* 597 U. S. 1, 70-71, 142 S.Ct. 2156 (2022).

In sum, the Court in *Heller* and *McDonald* recognized that the Second and Fourteenth Amendments protect the right of an ordinary, law-abiding citizen to possess a handgun in the home for self-defense. In *Buren,* the court further held that ordinary, law-abiding citizens have a similar right to carry handguns publicly for their self-defense. Thus, "the Second and Fourteenth Amendments protect an individual's right to carry a handgun for self-defense outside the home."[39]

The United States Supreme Court has yet to squarely address what types of weapons are "Arms" protected by the Second Amendment. As explained in *District of Columbia v. Heller,*[40] the Second Amendment's protection "extends, *prima facie*, to all instruments that constitute bearable arms, even those that were not in existence at the time of the founding." The Court also noted that "the Second Amendment does not protect those weapons not typically possessed by law-abiding citizens for lawful purposes,"[41] recognizing "the historical tradition of prohibiting the carrying of dangerous and unusual weapons."[42] But, "this minimal guidance is far from a comprehensive framework for evaluating restrictions on types of weapons, and it leaves open essential questions such as what makes a weapon 'bearable,' 'dangerous,' or 'unusual.'"[43]

In *State v. Bibbs,*[44] the court addressed a constitutional challenge to Hawaii's statutory ban on the possession of large-capacity magazines, or LCMs, for use with a pistol. Hawaii Revised Statutes (HRS) § 134-8(c) generally prohibits the manufacture, possession, or sale of detachable ammunition magazines that can hold more than ten rounds and be used with a pistol. Bibbs was convicted of, among other things, possessing a prohibited magazine in violation of this law. In this appeal he contended that his convictions cannot stand because HRS § 134-8(c) infringes on his right to bear arms, as protected by the Second Amendment to the United States Constitution. In rejecting this challenge, the court said:

---

[39] *New York State Rifle & Pistol Assn., Inc. v. Bruen*, 597 U. S. 1, 8-10, 142 S.Ct. 2122 (2022).

[40] *District of Columbia v. Heller*, 554 U.S. 570, 582, 128 S.Ct. 2783, 2792 (2008).

[41] *District of Columbia v. Heller*, 554 U.S. 570, 625, 128 S.Ct. 2783, 2816 (2008).

[42] *District of Columbia v. Heller*, 554 U.S. 570, 627, 128 S.Ct. 2783, 2817 (2008); *Caetano v. Massachusetts*, 577 U. S. 411, 417-419, 136 S.Ct. 1027, 194 L. Ed. 2d 99 (2016) (Alito, J., concurring in judgment)

[43] *Harrel v. Raoul*, 144 S.Ct. 2491, 2492 (2024) (THOMAS, J., concurring).

[44] *State v. Bibbs*, 2025 Haw. App. 451.

We hold that HRS § 134-8(c)'s prohibition on the possession of large-capacity magazines does not violate the Second Amendment. The Ninth Circuit recently concluded in an *en banc* opinion that California's similar ban on the possession of LCMs comports with the Second Amendment—in part because LCMs are neither "arms" nor accessories protected by the text of the Second Amendment.[45] Other courts have similarly concluded that the Second Amendment's text does not encompass the right to possess LCMs.[46] . . . In this case, Bibbs has not established that the Second Amendment's plain text protects his possession of a prohibited LCM.[47]

In *United States v. Rahimi*,[48] the United States Supreme Court addressed a federal statute that prohibits an individual subject to a domestic violence restraining order from possessing a firearm if that order includes a finding that the person "represents a credible threat to the physical safety of [an] intimate partner," or a child of the partner or individual.[49] Defendant Rahimi was subject to such an order. The question was whether this provision may be enforced against him consistent with the Second Amendment.[50]

The Court held that "[w]hen a restraining order contains a finding that an individual poses a credible threat to the physical safety of an intimate partner, that individual may—consistent with the Second Amendment—be banned from possessing firearms while the order is in effect. Since the founding, our Nation's firearm laws have included provisions preventing individuals who threaten physical harm to others from misusing firearms.[51] As applied to the facts of this case, wherein a

---

[45] *Duncan v. Bonta*, 133 F.4th 852, 860, 865, 869 (9th Cir. 2025).

[46] *See, e.g., Or. Firearms Fed'n v. Kotek*, 682 F. Supp. 3d 874, 911-13 (D. Or. 2023) (ruling that LCMs are not "arms" within the meaning of the Second Amendment); *Ocean State Tactical, LLC v. Rhode Island*, 646 F. Supp. 3d 368, 384-88 (D.R.I. 2022) (same), *aff'd on other grounds*, 95 F.4th 38 (1st Cir. 2024); *Brumback v. Ferguson*, No. 1:22-cv-03093-MKD, 2023 U.S. Dist. LEXIS 170819, 2023 WL 6221425, at *8 (E.D. Wash. Sept. 25, 2023) (same); *State v. Gator's Custom Guns, Inc.*, 586 P.3d 278, 283 (Wash. 2025) (same); *cf. Bevis v. City of Naperville*, 85 F.4th 1175, 1195 (7th Cir. 2023) (concluding for a related reason that LCMs are not protected "arms").

[47] *State v. Bibbs*, 2025 Haw. App. 451, at *2.

[48] *United States v. Rahimi*, 602 U.S. 680, 144 S.Ct. 1889 (2024).

[49] 18 *U. S.C.* §922(g)(8).

[50] *United States v. Rahimi*, 602 U.S. 680, 144 S.Ct. 1889, 1894 (2024).

[51] *United States v. Rahimi*, 602 U.S. 680, 144 S.Ct. 1889, 1896 (2024).

court found that the defendant posed a credible threat to the physical safety of the victim or her family, 18 *U.S.C.* § 922(g)(8) fits comfortably within the Nation's tradition of "preventing individuals who threatened physical harm to others from misusing firearms."[52]

---

§ 8.2. State court cases and issues

The Florida State Legislature, in Fla. Stat. § 790.335(1)(a), found and declared that:

> *The right of individuals to keep and bear arms is guaranteed under both the Second Amendment to the United States Constitution and § 8, Art. I of the State Constitution.*
>
> *§ 8(a) provides: "The right of the people to keep and bear arms in defense of themselves and of the lawful authority of the state shall not be infringed, except that the manner of bearing arms may be regulated by law."*
>
> *Florida's Right to Bear Arms*

(a) *New federalism*

When confronted with a conflict between federal constitutional law and state law provisions, a state is free, and indeed encouraged, to rely on its own constitution to provide greater protection to the privacy, liberty and property interests of its citizens than that afforded under parallel provisions of the federal Constitution. As a well-established principle of our federalist system, state constitutions may be the source of "individual liberties more expansive than those conferred by the federal Constitution."[53] This means that a state court is free as a matter of its own law to impose greater restrictions on government activity than those the United States Supreme Court holds to be necessary under federal constitutional standards.

---

[52] *United States v. Rahimi,* 602 U.S. 680, 144 S.Ct. 1889, 1896-97 (2024). Note also that in holding that Section 922(g)(8) is constitutional as applied to Rahimi, the Court rejected the Government's contention that Rahimi may be disarmed simply because he is not "responsible." Said the Court: "'Responsible' is a vague term. It is unclear what such a rule would entail." *Id.* at 1903.

[53] *Pruneyard Shopping Center v. Robins,* 447 U.S. 74, 81, 100 S.Ct. 2035, 2040 (1980).

The federal Constitution represents the baseline or "floor" of protection and, of course, a state may not drop below the federal floor;[54] it may, however, rely on its own state constitution to heighten that floor of protection. CAUTION: A state may establish, as a matter of its own law, a ceiling of protection for its citizens which may have the effect of placing additional restrictions upon, or requiring the exercise of additional precautions by, its officials.[55]

(b) *McDaniels v. State*

The Court, in *McDaniels v. State*,[56] held that Florida's Open Carry Ban, §790.053, Florida Statutes, violates the Second Amendment's right to bear arms in public. Said the court: "The Constitution protects the right to carry arms openly for self-defense. Florida's Open Carry Ban cannot be reconciled with that guarantee. Section 790.053, Florida Statutes, is therefore declared unconstitutional."

(c) *Burns v. State*

In *Burns v. State*,[57] the State "charged Burns with aggravated assault with a deadly weapon for his response to a verbal confrontation with a five-man tree-cutting crew that occurred in the yard of the home he leases as a residence for himself and his family, which includes his fiancée and her son. After one crew member made sexually suggestive gestures towards his fiancée and another waved a running chainsaw towards his dogs with the apparent threat to dismember them, Burns demanded that the crew members leave his property. Following their refusal to immediately leave, Burns retrieved his handgun from his residence and

---

[54] Note also that in *Timbs v. Indiana*, 586 U.S. 146, 149-50, 139 S.Ct. 682, 686-87 (2019), the United States Supreme Court held that the states cannot impose excessive fees, fines and forfeitures as criminal penalties. The Court's decision underscores that the Eighth Amendment's prohibition against "excessive fines" applies to states and localities as well as the federal government. Said the Court: "The Excessive Fines Clause is therefore incorporated by the Due Process Clause of the Fourteenth Amendment." *Id.*, 139 S.Ct. at 687.

[55] *See generally* Linde, *E. Pluribus—Constitutional Theory and State Courts,* 18 Ga. L. Rev. 165 (1984); Brennen, *State Constitutions and the Protection of Individual Rights,* 90 Harv. L. Rev. 489 (1977); Note, *The New Federalism, Toward a Principled Interpretation of the State Constitution,* 29 Stan. L. Rev. 297 (1977); Feldman & Abney, *The Double Security of Federalism: Protecting Individual Liberty Under the Arizona Constitution,* 20 Ariz. St. L.J. 115 (1988).

[56] *McDaniels v. State*, 2025 Fla.App. LEXIS 6846, ___ So.3d ___ (2025).

[57] *Burns v. State*, 361 So.3d 372 (4th Dist. 2023).

openly carried it in his yard while loading it by advancing a bullet into its chamber."[58]

In this appeal, the court declared:

> That a person's home is his or her "castle" is one of the most basic tenets of our jurisprudence.[59] However, for Richard Burns, charged with aggravated assault with a deadly weapon for openly carrying and loading his firearm in the yard of his own home, the "castle" our law entitled him to protect was relegated to a defenseless dungeon. We conclude that the trial court erred in denying his motion for immunity from prosecution pursuant to Florida's Stand Your Ground law.
>
> We therefore grant his petition . . . because he is legally entitled to immunity from prosecution on the aggravated assault charge.[60]

During the course of its decision, the *Burns* court explained:

> "Florida grants to all persons who have not been legally disqualified from owning, possessing, and using firearms not only an individual state constitutional right 'to keep and bear arms in defense of themselves,' Art. I, § 8(a), *Fla. Const.*, but also the statutory right 'to own, possess, and lawfully use' weapons, including firearms, at a person's 'home or place of business' without the restrictions against the open carrying of weapons or firearms imposed by section 790.053, Florida Statutes, or the requirements of a concealed carry license imposed by section 790.06, Florida Statutes.[61]

---

[58] *Burns v. State*, 361 So.3d 372, 375 (4th Dist. 2023).

[59] The "now-famous observation that 'the house of every one is to him as his castle and fortress, as well for his defence against injury and violence, as for his repose'" was first made by an English court in 1604. *See Wilson v. Lane*, 526 U.S. 603, 609-10, 119 S.Ct. 1692 (1999) (quoting *Semayne's Case*, (1604) 77 Eng. Rep. 194, 195 (KB)).

[60] *Burns v. State*, 361 So.3d 372, 375 (4th Dist. 2023).

[61] *See* Fla. Stat. § 790.25(3)(n) ("The provisions of §§ 790.053 and 790.06 do not apply in the following instances [inclusive of persons on their home property or place of business], and, despite such sections, it is lawful for [such persons] to own, possess, and lawfully use firearms and other weapons, ammunition, and supplies for lawful purposes [while on their home property or place of business as permitted by subsection (3)(n)][.]").

In other words, "Florida provides a statutory right to openly carry a weapon or firearm while on one's home property or place of business. Even when one is not at his or her home property or place of business, it is not unlawful in Florida to 'briefly and openly display' a lawfully carried firearm 'to the ordinary sight of another person,' so long as the firearm is not being 'intentionally displayed in an angry or threatening manner' when the display of the firearm is 'not in necessary self-defense.'[62] These statutes recognize that a firearm is not just a collector's item that is stored out-of-sight indefinitely. For a firearm to be useful for self-defense, it must be readily available and loaded, neither of which can be effectively and safely done if the firearm cannot be taken out of concealment or storage and openly displayed while being loaded and held."[63]

"As section 790.25(3)(n) permits, Burns had the right to openly carry the firearm he displayed and loaded because he was on his home property. Even if Burns had not been on his home property, it would not have been unlawful, as authorized by section 790.053(1), for him to 'briefly and openly display' his firearm in anticipation of possibly needing to use it for his and his fiancée's protection during his confrontation with the tree-cutting crew."[64]

Conclusion. "Openly carrying or displaying a firearm, and loading it by advancing a bullet in its chamber for it to be ready for use if needed, does not constitute the unjustified or threatened use of deadly force as a matter of law. Moreover, Burns had a lawful right to openly carry his firearm on his home property. Thus, Burns is entitled to immunity from prosecution for his non-deadly use of his firearm during the incident with the tree-cutting crew."[65]

---

[62] *See* FLA. STAT. § 790.053(1).

[63] *Burns v. State*, 361 So.3d 372, 377 (4th Dist. 2023).

[64] *Burns v. State*, 361 So.3d 372, 377 (4th Dist. 2023).

[65] *Burns v. State*, 361 So.3d 372, 378 (4th Dist. 2023) (citing FLA. STAT. § 776.032(1) (granting immunity from criminal prosecution for any use or threatened use of force permitted in § 776.012, § 776.013, or § 776.031.).

Notes

CHAPTER NINE
INSURANCE

Section

§ 9.1. Preliminary

Having insurance as a concealed carrier of firearms is important for several reasons, primarily because it offers financial and legal protection if you ever find yourself in a situation where you need to use your firearm for self-defense.

Even if you are fully justified in using your firearm for self-defense, you could still face legal challenges, including criminal prosecution or a civil lawsuit. Legal defense fees can quickly add up, and, without insurance, you might have to cover these costs out of pocket. Insurance for concealed carriers can help cover attorney fees, court costs, and other legal expenses, allowing you to focus on your defense rather than worrying about financial strain.

§ 9.2. Key aspects

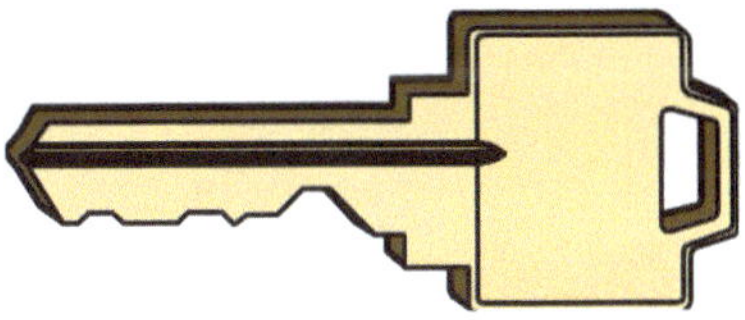

Here are several key aspects for the need for insurance:

1. It covers civil liability.

If you are involved in a self-defense shooting, you might be sued by the person you defended yourself against or their family. Even if you acted lawfully, a civil suit can be financially devastating. Concealed carry insurance can help protect you from these claims by covering damages, settlements, and court awards, ensuring your assets and livelihood are not put at risk.

2. It provides immediate legal assistance.

Many concealed carry insurance plans offer immediate access to a legal hotline you can call after an incident. This ensures that you get the right advice on both how to handle the situation and how to protect your rights from the very beginning. Having a lawyer who understands firearms law can make a significant difference in the outcome of your case.

3. It helps with bail and related expenses.

If you are arrested after a self-defense incident, insurance can help cover bail and related expenses, allowing you to get home to your family while you prepare for your legal defense. This can also include costs like expert witnesses, private investigators, and other support services that may be necessary for your case.

4. Access to education and training.

Some insurance providers also offer educational resources and training programs to their policyholders. This can include courses on the law, de-escalation, conflict avoidance, and situational awareness, which are invaluable skills for anyone carrying a concealed firearm. By becoming a better-informed and more responsible carrier, you can reduce the likelihood of ever needing to use your firearm.

5. Peace of mind.

Perhaps most importantly, having insurance gives you peace of mind. Knowing that you are financially and legally protected if the worst happens allows you to carry with confidence. You can be assured that if you ever have to defend yourself or your loved ones, you won't be alone in facing the potential fallout.

In sum, while no one ever wants to be in a situation where they need to draw their weapon, responsible concealed carry means being prepared for all possible outcomes. Insurance is a critical part of that preparedness, offering a safety net that ensures you have the support, resources, and protection you need to navigate any legal challenges that may arise.

We recommend 2A Legal. They have an emergency hotline 24 hours a day 365 days a year. *Visit:* https://2a-legal.com.

U.S. Law Shield is another option. *Visit:* https://ww2.uslawshield.com.

Chapter Ten
Case Studies

Cases
Doughty v. State
Gemmill v. State
State v. Valley
Gabriel v. State
Stuart v. State
Rivero v. State
Paese v. State

Doughty v. State

979 So.2d 1048 (Fla. 4th DCA 2008)

There was a near traffic collision between a motorcycle driven by Dan Doughty and an unmarked car occupied by three off-duty, out-of-state law enforcement officers. Doughty pulled up beside the car and said something to the effect of, "you almost ran me over," to which one of the officers responded, "you should not be driving in between traffic." The officers engaged in a verbal argument with Doughty until Doughty stated, "I have a gun, I'll kill you." He then lifted his shirt, reached into a leather pack that was around his waist, and grabbed what the officers believed was a weapon. The officers quickly exited the vehicle with their guns drawn, announced that they were police, and ordered Doughty to the ground. By the time the local police arrived, the officers had recovered a loaded .40 caliber Smith & Wesson handgun from Doughty's waist pack. Doughty was charged with carrying a concealed firearm without a permit.

QUESTION: Does the private conveyance exception of Fla. Stat § 790.25(3) permit the unlicensed carrying of a concealed firearm or other weapon in a zippered pack around the waist while riding a motorcycle?

ANSWER: NO. The private conveyance exception of Fla. Stat. § 790.25(5), by its express terms, applies only to the carrying of a

(Continued on the next page)

concealed weapon "within the interior of a private conveyance." Here, the court interpreted this language to require a person carrying a concealed weapon without a permit, while riding a motorcycle, to keep the concealed weapon securely encased and in an interior compartment of the motorcycle.

Under the facts presented, Doughty did not meet the statutory requirements of the private conveyance exception because, albeit he was traveling in a private conveyance and his firearm was securely encased, he was carrying the firearm on his person and did not have it within an interior compartment of his motorcycle.

Gemmill v. State

657 So.2d 900 (Fla. 4th DCA 1995)

Gemmill was stopped at a red light when his van was rear-ended by a one-ton truck carrying a front-end loader. Police responded to the scene of the accident, at which time Gemmill appeared incoherent, unable to answer questions, and unstable despite the use of a cane. The police thought Gemmill was drunk and became suspicious when he would not let anyone near his van. As it turns out, Gemmill has multiple cognitive and speech problems as a result of a previous scaffolding accident. Eventually, Gemmill moved his van out of traffic, requested medical attention, and was transported to the hospital by Emergency Medical Services for the alleged injuries sustained in the accident. Further police investigation revealed that Gemmill had a stun gun stored in a black waist pouch on his person. Officers also discovered a closed cardboard box (with a lid) wedged between the driver and passenger seat, which contained a small-caliber pistol.

Gemmill was charged (Count #1) with carrying a concealed firearm for the gun in the van and carrying a concealed weapon for the stun gun found in Gemmill's waist pouch (Count #2).

QUESTION: Should this case go to court, what is the likely result?

ANSWER: Fla. Stat. § 790.01(2) makes it a crime to carry a concealed firearm on or about the person. However, § 790.25(5) provides an exception to § 790.01(2), and states, in pertinent part: "Notwithstanding subsection (2), it is lawful and is not a violation of § 790.01 to possess a concealed firearm or other weapon for self-defense or other lawful purpose within the interior of a private conveyance, without a license, if the firearm or other weapon is securely encased or is otherwise not readily accessible for immediate use."

(Continued on the next page)

"Securely encased" is defined as: "in a glove compartment, whether or not locked; snapped in a holster; in a gun case, whether or not locked; in a zippered gun case; or in a *closed box or container which requires a lid or cover to be opened for access.* FLA. STAT. § 790.001(16).

As to count one, since Gemmill's gun was securely encased as it was contained in a closed box which required a lid or cover to be opened for access, his possession of the firearm was lawful.

As to count two, the stun gun in Gemmill's leather waist pouch, the court said: Here, Gemmill was carrying a concealed weapon on his waist in a securely encased zippered pack, inside an automobile. Section 790.25 specifically provides that the securely encased exception does not legalize the carrying of a concealed weapon on the person.

State v. Valley

381 So. 3d 633 (Fla. 2nd DCA 2024)

John Valley was pulled over by police officers for a traffic infraction. When the officers approached the car, they observed a handgun in the car's glove box and smelled the odor of burnt marijuana. They asked Valley to get out of the car. Valley was wearing a crossbody pack over his shoulder and chest that was zipped closed. When the officers removed the pack and searched it, they discovered a loaded handgun. They then arrested Valley for carrying a concealed firearm in violation of Fla. Stat. § 790.01(2). Valley filed a motion to dismiss, arguing that under § 790.25(5), he was permitted to possess the concealed firearm because it had been securely encased within a private conveyance.

Fla. Stat. § 790.01(2) provides in pertinent part:

> **Possession in private conveyance.—** [It] is lawful . . . for a person 18 years of age or older to possess a concealed firearm or other weapon for self-defense or other lawful purpose within the interior of a private conveyance, without a license, if the firearm or other weapon is securely encased or is otherwise not readily accessible for immediate use. Nothing herein contained prohibits the carrying of a legal firearm other than a handgun anywhere in a private conveyance when such firearm is being carried for a lawful use. ***Nothing herein contained shall be construed to authorize the carrying of a concealed firearm or other weapon on the person.*** This subsection shall be liberally construed in favor of the lawful use, ownership, and possession of firearms and other weapons, including lawful self-defense as provided in § 776.012. [Emphasis added.]

On appeal, the court rejected Valley's contention that as long as the firearm was securely encased, he could lawfully possess it anywhere in the vehicle—even on his person—because the statute does not limit the exception to constructive possession. "This interpretation," held the court, "is inconsistent with the plain language of § 790.25(5), which expressly limits the right to possess a firearm in a vehicle to those that are either securely encased or not otherwise available for immediate use and not carried on the person." The statute does not allow possession on the person.

Gabriel v. State

2024 Fla.App., No. 4D2024-1502

Mr. Gabriel was walking his small dog when a large pit bull came around the corner of a building, made threatening sounds and moved toward Gabriel and his dog. Gabriel tried to kick the pit bull away, which caused the pit bull to become even more aggressive. He then tried to scare the pit bull away by firing warning shots with a gun over the pit bull's head, but the pit bull continued to attack, pinning Gabriel and his dog into a corner. At this point, Gabriel shot and killed the pit bull.

The pit bull's owner, who had been walking the pit bull without a leash, then came around the corner of the building. Gabriel provided his version of the events to the pit bull's owner and then left.

QUESTION: If the state files charges related to cruelty to animals and discharging a firearm in a residential area, should Mr. Gabriel make a motion to dismiss the prosecution based the Stand Your Ground (SYG) defense of immunity from prosecution under FLA. STAT. § 776.012(2) (providing for the justifiable use of deadly force in defense of person), and FLA. STAT. § 776.032 (providing for immunity from prosecution under the "Stand Your Ground" law).

ANSWER: YES. Even though the state opposed Mr. Gabriel's attempt to assert SYG immunity from prosecution, arguing that the statutory language authorizes deadly force only by a person *against another person* and does not apply to the use of deadly force against *an animal*, the court held otherwise.

Under Florida law, *deadly force in defense of person* is authorized when "necessary to prevent imminent death or great bodily harm to himself or herself or another" or "to prevent the imminent commission of a forcible felony." FLA. STAT. § 776.012(2). The use of the deadly force provision does not include language that the force must always be used against a person. Thus, the court concluded that §776.012(2) authorizes deadly force against an animal when the person using or threatening to use the force "believes such force is necessary to prevent imminent death or great bodily harm to himself or herself or another."

Stuart v. State

772 So.2d 865 (Fla. 2d DCA 1996)

QUESTION: Does waving a gun in the air amount to the use of deadly force?

ANSWER: NO. Waving a gun in the air does not amount to the use of deadly force. By contrast, firing a firearm in the vicinity of human beings constitutes the use of deadly force as a matter of law. *See Miller v. State*, 613 So. 2d 530, 531 (Fla. 3d DCA 1993).

Rivero v. State

871 So.2d 953 (Fla. 2004)

QUESTION: Mr. Rivero pointed a gun at a person without firing it. Is this the use of deadly force?

ANSWER: NO. The use-of-force statute looks to the amount of force that is actually used. "Pointing a firearm (without firing it) amounts to the use of nondeadly force." In this case, since Mr. Rivero pointed the gun without firing it, this was nondeadly force, which then became a jury question as to whether it was the "justifiable use of nondeadly force." In this regard, FLA. STAT. § 776.012 provides:

> **§ 776.012. Use or threatened use of force in defense of person.**
>
> **(1)** A person is justified in using or threatening to use force, except deadly force, against another when and to the extent that the person reasonably believes that such conduct is necessary to defend himself or herself or another against the other's imminent use of unlawful force. A person who uses or threatens to use force in accordance with this subsection does not have a duty to retreat before using or threatening to use such force.

Note, however, that the pointing of a firearm at or in the direction of another may violate FLA. STAT. § 784.011, which provides that a person who assaults another person commits a misdemeanor of the second degree. In this regard, an "assault" is defined as "an intentional, unlawful threat by word or act to do violence to the person of another, coupled with an apparent ability to do so, and doing some act which creates a well-founded fear in such other person that such violence is imminent.

Paese v. State

381 So.3d 4 (Fla. 4th DCA 2024)

Ms. Paese was a resident of a high-rise condominium complex. One of the condo's elevators opens into Paese's private unit with a key fob that provides her with exclusive access. The facts of this case unfolded when she threw a roll of duct tape into the interior of the elevator after four men used a "master" key fob to override her exclusive access by stopping on her floor and opening the elevator door that separates the elevator's interior from Paese's unit. Paese threw the roll of tape from within the interior of her unit and in the direction of the four men who were standing in the open elevator as the elevator rested at the private landing for her unit.

When Paese first observed the four men in the open elevator, one of them had extended his arm into an area described as a "foyer" to hold the elevator door open. That individual was the condominium's property manager, whom Paese knew. Paese did not know the other three men. Thereafter, Paese saw one of the four men raise his cell phone to begin taking photographs of the interior of her unit. That man was the code inspector alleged to be Paese's victim. At the time, he was not in uniform and had not shown his code inspector's badge at any point during the incident, nor did he verbally identify himself to her.

Paese was "shocked" when she saw the four men, none of whom she was expecting at that time, in the open elevator. In fact, Paese had notified the men not to come to her unit before they suddenly appeared in the open elevator at the threshold of her unit, taking pictures of the interior of her home despite the undisputed fact that she never gave permission for any of the men to open the elevator door at the private landing that provides exclusive access to her unit.

Pease yelled for the men to leave, but they refused. At this point, Paese reached into the elevator and swatted the alleged victim's cell phone out of his hand, knocking it to the elevator's floor. The property manager then removed his extended arm and ended the encounter. This constituted the extent of the altercation, and the code inspector suffered no physical injuries in the incident.

(Continued on the next page)

It was established at court that Paese's key fob provides her exclusive access to her unit, and it does not provide her with access to any other unit or foyer. And, it is only programmed for her side of the elevator, on her floor. According to the property manager, however, her foyer is considered a "limited common element" of the condo.

QUESTION: Can a high-rise condominium dweller, consistent with Florida's Stand Your Ground ("SYG") law, use non-deadly force to prevent or terminate the tortious interference with her personal property?

ANSWER: YES. Ms. Paese is entitled to immunity from prosecution because her use of non-deadly force to prevent or terminate the tortious interference with her personal property was consistent with the level of authorized force permitted by FLA. STAT. § 776.032(1), the SYG law.

RATIONALE: "Whether a defendant was justified in using a particular level of force against another must be evaluated in accordance with 'the objective, reasonable person standard.' . . . Under that standard, the legal question to be resolved in all SYG cases is whether 'a reasonable and prudent person in the same position as the defendant would believe' that the level of authorized force used was 'necessary' to prevent the harm or offense for which such force is statutorily permitted." *Id.* at 12.

The plain language of § 776.031(1) "authorizes the use of non-deadly force to prevent or terminate the tortious or criminal interference with one's personal property." And here, it is "undisputed that Paese did not consent to the property manager's use of a master key fob to gain elevator access to her unit's private landing and foyer for the purpose of allowing the code inspector to photograph the interior of her home. Moreover, for purposes of her condo, "limited common elements" are statutorily defined as "elements which are reserved for the use of a certain unit . . . to the exclusion of all other units, as specified in the declaration." § 718.103(19).

(Continued on the next page)

"Moreover, because the foyer was 'reserved' for Paese's exclusive use, she had the right to keep her secondary door open at any time. Therefore, Paese would have had an expectation of privacy and the right to the quiet enjoyment of her property regardless of whether the secondary door was open or removed because an open secondary door is no different than a removed secondary door." *Id.* at 13.

"Because section 776.031(1) permits the proportionate use of nondeadly force 'to prevent or terminate' the 'tortious or criminal interference' with 'personal property,' Paese was justified in using such force[.]" The court concluded, therefore, that "pursuant to section 776.031(1), it was objectively reasonable for Paese to perceive the four men's unauthorized use of a master key fob to override her exclusive access and intrude upon her private home while taking unwelcomed photographs of its interior, including the personal property in her home, as the tortious interference with her personal property that she could justifiably prevent or terminate with the proportionate use of non-deadly force—*i.e.*, by throwing the roll of duct tape towards the open elevator and swatting the cell phone out of the alleged victim's hand." *Id.* at 14-15.

Notes

Chapter Eleven
Frequently Asked Questions (FAQs)

Q: What to do when you see the No Guns Allowed Sign.

A: This is a complex question, and there are multiple answers. Let's start with the basics.

- Don't go inside.
- Safely stow your gun in the car and then enter.
- Enter at your own risk, taking a mental note of the sign.

"No Firearm" signs in Florida have no force of law unless they are posted on property that is specifically mentioned in State Law as being off limits to those with a Permit/License to Carry.

Q: Can you carry a concealed firearm in a bank?

A: Yes. If the bank has a no gun sign, please follow the suggestion above.

Q: Can you carry a concealed firearm in a restaurant with a bar?

A: It Depends. If the establishment is more restaurant than bar, you may. However, if it's a bar that happens to serve food, you may not.

Let's dive a little deeper. You may not under any circumstances sit at the bar or a table within the bar area. If you must walk near the bar area to use the restroom, this is allowable with caution. Do not get sidetracked or open conversations with individuals within the bar area. You are to use the restroom and avoid the bar area to the best of your ability. Consuming any alcohol while carrying concealed is frowned upon.

Q: What about carrying concealed near a school, for example, picking your child up or meeting them at the corner.

A: A person with a concealed carry license from the state where the school is located can possess a firearm within 1,000 feet of the school. Carpool lines and outer perimeter meetups are ok, being mindful of distance.

Q: I am planning a family trip to Disney World; can I carry concealed on their property?

A: NO! You will be escorted off the property or possibly arrested. Firearms are not permitted at the Disney Resort, including the theme parks, Downtown Disney District, and resort hotels. This includes ammunition, knives, and any other type of weapon. Disney also prohibits any toys that look like weapons, such as toy guns, toy blasters, and squirt guns.

Disney security searches all bags and may confiscate any prohibited items, and there is no holding area for prohibited items.

Other items that are not permitted at Disney include: pepper spray, mace, stun guns, handcuffs, zip ties, box cutters, razor blades, and duct tape.

Visit: https://disneyworld.disney.go.com/faq/resorts/guns-weapons

Q: Can I carry concealed to my doctor's appointment?

A: If the physician or their group owns the building, they can post a sign; if the physician rents space in a building, they can't prohibit concealed carry with signage. Only the property owner can do that. Regarding signage, follow the protocol mentioned earlier.

Q: Can I carry concealed at my Church or Synagogue service?

A: Yes, there is no issue with this. Also, the law currently states that if a church shares a property with a school, it is permissible.

Q: Can I carry my gun into an airport?

A: Generally, no. Airports, including those in Florida, are regulated by both federal and state laws. Under Florida law, bringing a weapon into the airport is a second-degree misdemeanor punishable by up to 60 days in jail, with a maximum fine of $500.

It is, however, a defense that you properly checked all firearms as baggage in accordance with law, or were authorized by a federal agency or the airport operator to possess the firearm in a secured area. It is also a defense if you possessed, at the screening checkpoint for the secured area, a handgun that you were licensed to carry and exited the screening checkpoint for the secured area immediately upon completion of the required screening processes and notification that you possessed the handgun.

In addition, it is important to be aware of the Transportation Security Administration (TSA) rules. According to TSA:

- "You may transport unloaded firearms in a locked hard-sided container as checked baggage only. Declare the firearm and/or ammunition to the airline with your other checked bags at the ticket counter. The container must completely secure the firearm and prevent it from being accessed. Locked cases that can be easily opened are not permitted."[66] The case you use should be specifically designed to secure firearms during transport. The hard-sided gun case must be sturdy enough to maintain its shape even with a heavy weight on top of it.

- In addition, firearms "must be unloaded and locked in a hard-sided container and transported as checked baggage only." As defined by 49 *C.F.R.* § 1540.5, a loaded firearm has a live round of ammunition, or any component thereof, in the chamber or cylinder or in a magazine inserted in the firearm. For civil enforcement purposes, TSA also considers a firearm to be loaded when both the firearm and ammunition are accessible to the passenger. For example, if an individual has a firearm in accessible baggage and ammunition in his/her pocket, or any combination where the individual has access to both, the firearm is considered 'loaded' for purposes of assessing a civil penalty. Only the passenger should retain the key or combination to the lock unless TSA personnel request the key to open the firearm container to ensure compliance with TSA regulations. You may use any brand or type of lock to secure your firearm case, including TSA-recognized locks."[67]

---

[66] https://www.tsa.gov/travel/transporting-firearms-and-ammunition

[67] https://www.tsa.gov/travel/transporting-firearms-and-ammunition

- Bringing an unloaded firearm with accessible ammunition to the security checkpoint carries the same civil penalty/fine as bringing a loaded firearm to the checkpoint.
- Firearm parts, including magazines, clips, bolts, and firing pins, must be transported in checked baggage.
- Replica firearms, including firearm replicas that are toys, may be transported in checked baggage only.
- Rifle scopes are permitted in carry-on and checked baggage.
- Ammunition may only be transported in checked baggage.
- Firearm magazines and ammunition clips, whether loaded or empty, must be securely boxed or included within a hard-sided case containing an unloaded firearm. Read the requirements governing the transport of ammunition in checked baggage as defined by 49 *C.F.R.* § 175.10(a)(8).
- Small arms ammunition (up to .75 caliber and shotgun shells of any gauge) must be packaged in a fiber (such as cardboard), wood, plastic, or metal box specifically designed to carry ammunition and declared to your airline.
- Ammunition may be transported in the same hard-sided, locked case as a firearm if it has been packed as described above. You cannot use firearm magazines or clips for packing ammunition unless they completely enclose the ammunition. Firearm magazines and ammunition clips, whether loaded or empty, must be boxed or included within a hard-sided, locked case. Please check with your airline for quantity limits for ammunition.[68]

Q: Can I Be Armed on an Airplane?

A: NO. You can't be armed with a firearm while on an airplane. The only people who may qualify to carry firearms on planes are qualified law enforcement personnel, trained air marshals, pilots, and crewmembers of passenger and cargo aircraft who have completed the required training.

---

[68] https://www.tsa.gov/travel/transporting-firearms-and-ammunition

Q: What is the penalty if I make a mistake when bringing my firearm?

A: Mistakes when flying with a gun can be costly, and you could face both civil and criminal charges. Per TSA on their site: ". . . local and state governments, and other countries, may have their own rules on firearm possession or transportation. As a result, prohibited items may result in both a TSA civil enforcement action and a criminal enforcement action." TSA "may impose civil penalties of up to $14,950 per violation per person", and repeat violations have even higher penalties.

Q: Can I carry a concealed weapon on the Tri-Rail or Brightline Train?

A: Just like airports, this is also illegal.

In Florida, it is against the law to conceal carry a firearm in certain places: police stations, jails, prisons, courthouses, polling places, schools, colleges, airports, meetings of governing bodies, and any area where federal law prohibits carrying firearms; essentially, most government buildings, educational institutions, and areas where alcohol is the primary focus of the establishment.

Q: Is firing a *warning shot* always permitted?

A: NO: The firing of a warning shot is considered the use of deadly force under Florida law.

Q: Is the pointing of a firearm in the direction of another person considered an "aggravated assault"?

A: YES. The pointing of a firearm in the direction of another person may be considered an "aggravated assault with a deadly weapon."

First, Fla. Stat. § 784.011(1) defines an assault as an "intentional, unlawful threat by word or act to do violence to the person of another, coupled with an apparent ability to do so, and doing some act which creates a well-founded fear in such other person that such violence is imminent." Building upon that, § 784.021(1) defines an "aggravated assault" as an assault with "a deadly weapon without intent to kill."

As the Florida Standard Jury Instruction (8.2) provides: To prove the crime of Aggravated Assault, the State must prove the following four elements beyond a reasonable doubt: (1) The defendant intentionally and unlawfully threatened, either by word or act, to do violence to (victim); (2) At the time (defendant) appeared to have the ability to carry out the threat; (3) The act of (defendant) created in the mind of (victim) a well-founded fear that the violence was about to take place; and (4) The assault was made with a deadly weapon.

Q: What happens if I'm stopped by the police for a minor traffic violation and I have a gun on me or in my car?

A: In most states, including Florida, you are not legally required to inform the police officer that you have a concealed firearm unless the officer specifically asks you or if you are taken into custody. However, it's essential to know the specific laws in your state, as they can vary.

If the officer does ask, the best approach is to calmly inform them that you have a concealed carry permit and ask if they would like to see your license. Keep your hands visible and move slowly to avoid any misunderstandings.

If they do not ask, there is no legal requirement to advise them of the presence of your firearm. Obviously, blurting out, "I have a gun," especially if you're nervous, could unintentionally escalate a routine traffic stop into a more serious situation. Stay calm, respectful, and cooperative. If the officer has any concerns, he or she will address them directly.

Many officers polled suggest that when initially handing over your license, registration, and insurance, you should also hand over your carry permit. This alerts the officer in a calm and respectful way that you may have a firearm in the vehicle. Note also that if the police officer does a computer check on you during the traffic stop, the "look up" may indicate that you have a carry permit.

Q: Is open carry permitted?

A: YES: In light of *McDaniels v. State,* open carry is now allowed in Florida. The court ruled that Florida's Open Carry Ban, §790.053, Florida Stat., violates the Second Amendment's right to bear arms in public.

Q: Can anyone get a firearm without a background check?

A: NO. The revised provisions in Florida's law do not change who can purchase a firearm or the waiting period to purchase a firearm.

Q: Can you now carry a firearm anywhere in Florida?

A: NO. There is a comprehensive list of prohibited places where you cannot carry a firearm set forth in FLA. STAT. § 790.06(12)(a).

Q: Is hollow-point ammunition lawful to have in Florida? (Question submitted by a person who has recently moved here from New Jersey).

A: YES. Hollow-point ammo is allowed.

Q: What Ammunition is illegal in Florida?

A: The State of Florida does not regulate hollow-point ammunition, however, under Florida law, ***the following types of ammunition are illegal in Florida***: armor-piercing, exploding ammunition, dragon's breath shotgun shells, bolo shells, or flechette shells. These types of ammunition are found at:

- **Armor-piercing bullet, FLA. STAT. § 790.31 (a)**
- **Exploding bullet, FLA. STAT. § 790.31 (b)**
- **Dragon's Breath, FLA. STAT. § 790.31 (d)**
- **Bolo Shell, FLA. STAT. § 790.31 (e)**
- **Flechette Shell, FLA. STAT. § 790.31 (f)**

The law further provides, at § 790.31(2)(b), that possession of such items is a *felony of the third degree.* Possession with the intent to use such items to assist in the commission of a criminal act is a *felony of the second degree.*

Q: For gun owners, is voting important?

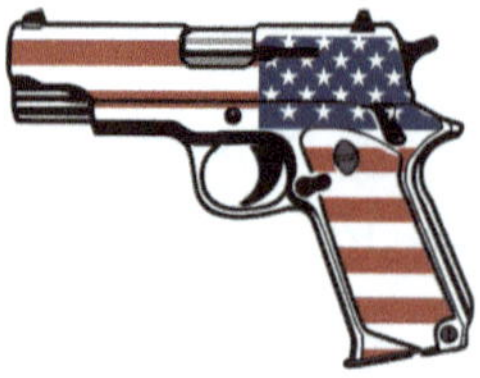

A: YES! For some reason, too many gun owners and enthusiasts do not vote. Protect and exercise your constitutional *right to vote* in local, state, and nationwide elections, *especially when Second Amendment rights are at stake!*

Appendix -A-
The Ten Commandments of Gun Ownership

Commandment 1. ***Treat Every Firearm as if It's Loaded.***

This rule is non-negotiable. Even if you are certain your gun is unloaded, always double-check that and handle it with care, and assume it could fire. This mindset helps prevent accidents by ingraining safe handling habits.

Commandment 2. ***Never forget Commandment #1.***

Commandment 3. ***Keep Your Finger Off the Trigger Until Ready to Shoot.***

It's essential to maintain control over your firearm and avoid placing your finger on the trigger until you are fully prepared to take a shot. This helps prevent unintentional discharge, which could have tragic consequences.

Commandment 4. ***Never Point Your Gun at Anything You Don't Intend to Destroy.***

This rule goes together with treating your firearm as if it's always loaded. Whether you're at home, at the range, or out carrying, always be mindful of where the gun is pointed. Safe directions mean there's no risk of harming others or damaging property.

Commandment 5. ***Secure Your Firearm Properly When Not in Use.***

The most crucial aspect of gun safety at home is secure storage. A firearm should always be locked up when not in use. Consider:

• *Gun safes:* A sturdy, tamper-proof safe is the best option for securing your firearms. Look for models with reliable locking mechanisms and consider biometric or digital locks for added convenience. *Biometric safes* open with your fingerprint, ensuring rapid access in emergencies. They combine quick access with high security. The goal is to make sure that only authorized individuals can access the gun.

• *Gun lock boxes:* Smaller than a full-sized safe, these are perfect for storing a handgun. They're ideal if you need to secure a firearm quickly but still have it accessible when necessary.

• *Trigger locks & cable locks:* These inexpensive devices can be used to block the trigger or action of a firearm, rendering it unusable until the lock is removed. While they don't provide the same level of security as a safe, they can act as an extra layer of protection.

Commandment 6. *Store Ammunition Separately.*

Whenever possible, keep your ammunition stored in a different location from your firearm. This adds an additional level of safety, ensuring that unauthorized users can't quickly make a firearm operational if they do manage to access it.

Commandment 7. *Educate Family Members About Firearm Safety.*

If you live with others, especially children, it's important to teach them about gun safety. Let them know that firearms are not toys, and they should never be touched without your explicit permission. Explain the dangers and encourage open communication so that if they ever come across a gun, they know to inform an adult immediately.

Commandment 8. *Regularly Inspect Your Security Measures.*

Make a habit of checking your safes, locks, and storage solutions. Ensure everything is in good working order and hasn't been tampered with. Your security measures are only effective if they're reliable.

Commandment 9. *De-escalation First When Possible.*

Don't let your ego dictate your actions. One of the most important skills as a responsible concealed carrier is the ability to de-escalate a situation. If someone's words or behavior is pushing your buttons, remember that you and you alone are in control of your emotions. Don't let pride or anger turn a verbal exchange into a violent confrontation. The goal is to avoid conflict whenever possible, and the best way to do that is by staying calm, composed, and level-headed. Even when dealing with road rage, the best place for the aggressive driver is in front of you. Simply let them pass and move on with your day.

Commandment 10. *Think About Everyone's Safety.*

When carrying or using a firearm, you have a responsibility not just to yourself, but to everyone around you, including bystanders. It's not enough to think about what's directly in front of the gun; you need to be aware of where a bullet could travel beyond your target. Make it a habit to assess your surroundings, consider your angles and line of sight, and always have a mental plan. Thinking ahead can save lives, prevent accidents, and ensure that you act with the utmost care and responsibility. By adhering to these ***Ten Commandments of Gun Ownership***, you are not only protecting yourself but also everyone around you.

Notes

APPENDIX -B-
HEALTH AND FITNESS

Eye Health

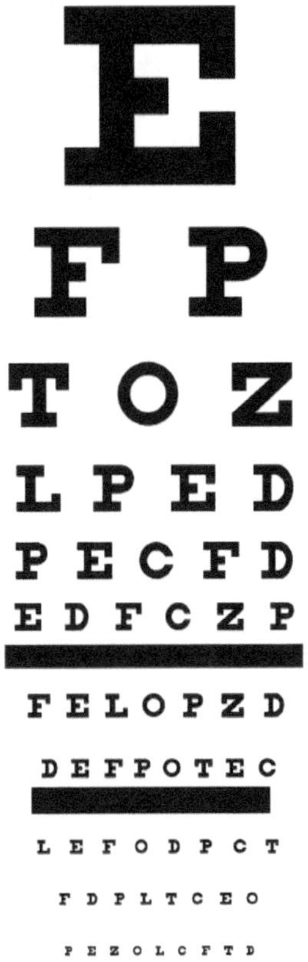

Eye health is something that is often overlooked, but it plays a crucial role in many aspects of life, including the safe and effective use and handling of firearms. As we age, our eyesight can change gradually, sometimes without us even realizing it. That's why it's important to schedule regular annual eye exams to ensure your vision is at its best. A small difference in clarity can make a significant impact, from blurry to sharp, or from missing important details to seeing them clearly.

When it comes to concealed carry, sharp vision isn't just about being able to read road signs or see far-off objects; it's about safety and accuracy. If your vision is compromised, your ability to accurately identify targets, read your surroundings, or even assess potential threats can be affected. Squinting with your dominant eye to get a clear view, while your non-dominant eye is most likely closed (unless you're using an optic), is not an ideal way to handle a firearm. You want to be able to see clearly and respond quickly, without any delay or distraction caused by poor eyesight.

Think of it this way: your firearm is only as effective as your ability to use it properly. If your vision is impaired, it compromises your accuracy, reaction time, and overall awareness of your environment. Regular eye exams can help you stay ahead of any vision changes, ensuring you are always prepared to see clearly and act confidently. If you need glasses or contact lenses, consider getting lenses that are suited for different lighting conditions, and make sure to have backup options if you carry frequently.

Don't let something as simple as blurry vision hinder your ability to protect yourself. Prioritize your eye health just as you would prioritize regular practice and training with your firearm. Clear vision is an essential part of responsible and safe concealed carry.

Physical Fitness: Why It Matters for Concealed Carry

Everyone has a different level of physical fitness, and that's okay. What's important is to do the best you can within your capabilities and to aim for improvement where possible. Elevating your fitness level, or at least maintaining it, can enhance your reaction time, strength, confidence, and endurance—all crucial aspects when it comes to responsible concealed carry.

Think about it: a quicker reaction time can mean the difference between staying safe and being caught off guard. Strength and endurance can help you stay steady, maintain control of your firearm, and move efficiently if a situation requires it. Confidence in your physical abilities can boost your mental readiness, making you more prepared to handle stressful situations.

So how can you work on your fitness, even if you're starting from scratch? Here are a few ideas:

- ***Get Moving:*** Whether it's getting in your daily steps, riding a bike, or taking a brisk walk, find an activity that keeps you active and do it consistently.

- ***Strength Training, a.k.a., weightlifting or resistance training:*** You don't need to lift heavy weights to build strength. Start with simple exercises like push-ups (even modified ones), sit-ups, or bodyweight squats. You can gradually increase the difficulty as you get stronger. As we age, strength training can reduce the risk of chronic diseases like arthritis, heart disease, and diabetes. It can also help with weight control, improve sleep, and reduce depression. Also, in older adults, regular strengthening exercises will help prevent osteoporosis and frailty by stimulating the growth of muscle and bone.

- ***Flexibility and Balance:*** Consider trying yoga, a Pilates class, or going to a "stretch zone." Flexibility and balance are often overlooked but can make a big difference in your overall physical readiness.

- ***Explore Fitness Apps or Personal Training:*** If you're unsure where to start, try instructional fitness apps that guide you through routines, or hire a personal trainer if it fits your budget. They can help create a personalized plan tailored to your goals and abilities.

- ***Eat Smart, Enjoy Life:*** Physical fitness isn't just about exercise; it's also about making smart food choices. Eating a balanced diet fuels your body and helps you stay energized, without feeling deprived of the joys of life.

These are all just suggestions, but we'd be doing you a disservice if we didn't mention them in this guide. Self-discipline in maintaining your physical health can improve your life in countless ways, from everyday tasks to staying alert and ready when carrying concealed.

What if this is your wake-up call to prioritize your fitness? Even small steps can lead to big changes, and those changes can make a real difference when it comes to your safety, confidence, and overall well-being. Take it one step at a time, and remember, every little bit helps.

Notes

Appendix -C-
Gun Care And Maintenance

Maintaining your firearm is a crucial part of concealed carry. If you allow buildup from range use or lack of lubrication to occur, you could be inadvertently causing your sidearm to become unreliable. In this Appendix, we provide various ideas of what products we use and recommend. In addition to the basic kits sold at stores, there is a diverse market of choices. Over the course of many years, we have chosen specific products to keep our firearms in tip-top condition.

One question needs to be answered: *Do I need to clean my gun after each use?* The answer is a simple ***yes.*** Don't allow lead built-up and dirt to ruin your firearm, or worse, cause it to misfire.

A few suggestions may be found below. You must, however, choose what is right for you or recommended by the manufacturer for your specific firearm.

The above collection includes:

- Basic Kit for the caliber, in this case 9mm. (rod & barrel brush)
- Nitrile Gloves with grip
- Gun Mat is the perfect surface to work on
- Disposable brushes to be replaced after the bristles wear (removes hardened residue)
- Cotton Gun Wipes (a medium thickness is recommended). Cut-up t-shirts are an option
- Hoppes Number 9 Gun Cleaner
- TW 25 Lubricant in 12cc Syringe (Perfect for the Grooves in the Slide, doesn't drip)
- Slip 2000 Gun Lube (parts that require a thin coat of oil)
- Bore Stix and extra-long swabs

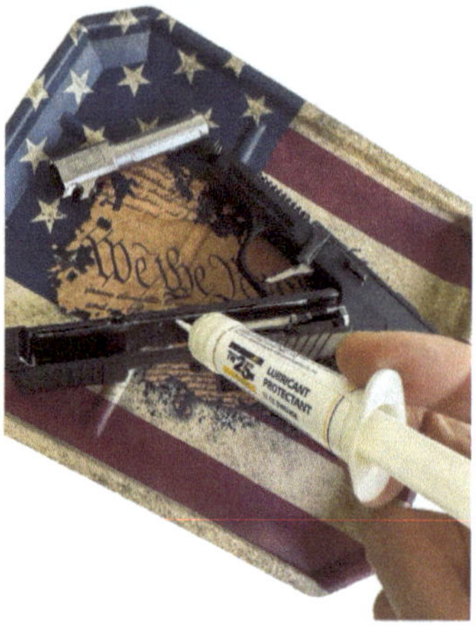

Obviously, there are numerous cleaning and lubricating products on the market. The goal is to pick what works best for you. Here is another example:

Speak to ten different gun enthusiasts, and you will hear ten different suggestions for cleaning. For specifics on "how" to clean, there are numerous websites.[69] For specific items needed, here are a few basics:

- **Cleaning rod.** Cleaning rods have a tough nylon coating that will not scratch the rifling of the firearm's barrel. If your rod has a rotating handle, it may give you some better positive control. Bore rods are sold in different lengths, so you will need to take into account the barrel and receiver length of your weapon.

- **A cleaning brush.** Some brushes do not remove carbon buildup well. That is why some use a nylon brush instead of a brass brush. The nylon one is less abrasive. Also consider a gun toothbrush. Besides the one in your bathroom, Hoppe's Utility Brush is great for cleaning out slide grooves and trigger parts.

- **A jag or loop.** This is the little attachment that goes on the end of a cleaning rod to facilitate the use of a cleaning patch.

---

[69] Here are just a few:
www.pelican.com/us/en/discover/pelican-flyer/post/how-to-clean-a-gun-in-6-steps
www.hoppes.com/ho-blog-new-gun-owners/ho-blog-5-steps-to-proper-handgun-cleaning.html
www.youtube.com/watch?app=desktop&v=dMNcqrIGEpw

• **Patches.** Patches are designed to help you clean with 360-degree coverage. They may also be used to wipe off extra cleaning fluid or oil.

• **Gun cleaning cotton swabs.** Use these to get every last piece of grim and debris out of chambers, slides, receivers, magazine housing, sights and bolts.

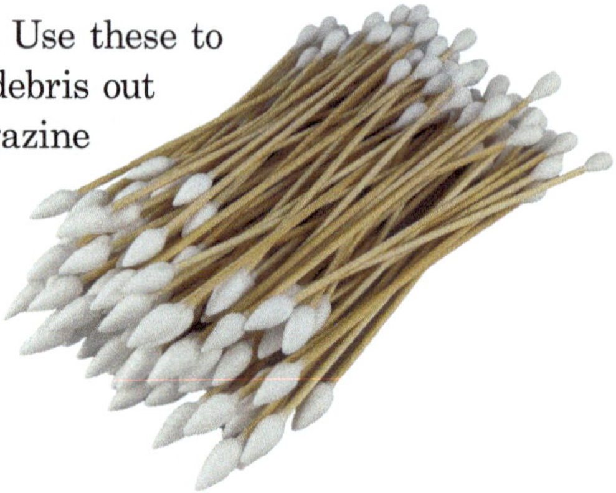

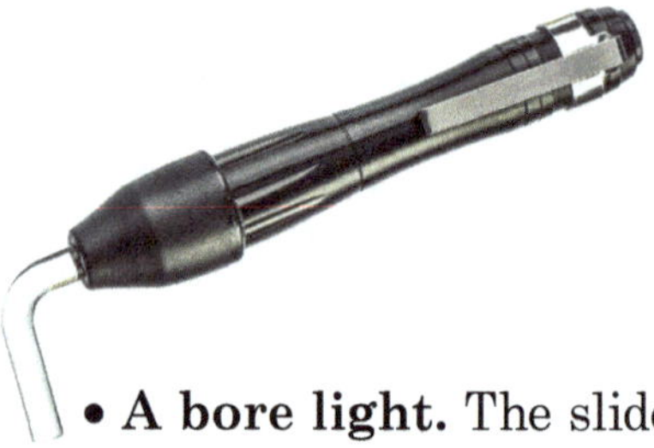

• **A bore light.** The slide-on fiber-optic acrylic piece is perfect for illuminating the interior of firearm barrels to spot scratches or debris.

• **Cleaning fluid.** There are four different types of fluids used to clean a gun. Each has its own mission.

  ○ *Solvents* remove carbon, lead, and other residue from the bore. For routine quick cleanings ,use a bore snake, running it through with a small amount of bore cleaner.

  ○ *Degreasers* remove existing dirt and oil from the moving parts of the firearm, creating a fresh, clean surface.

  ○ *Lubricants* provide protection against rust and, guess what, they lubricate.

  ○ *Protectants* should be considered if your gun will be exposed to harsh or very wet conditions.

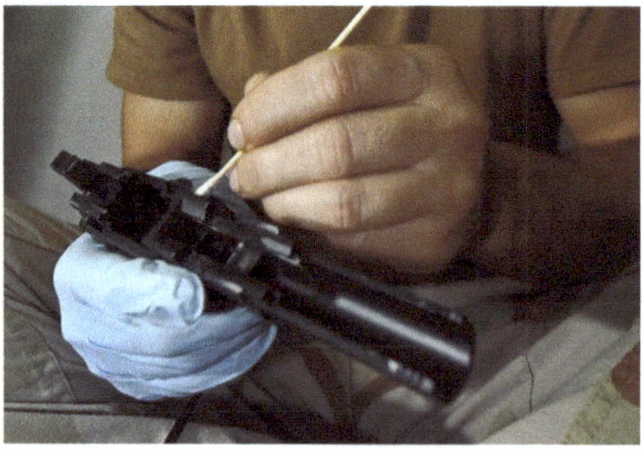

Table of Cases

(All References Are to Pages in This Text)

Notes